Bridging America's Skills Gap

Mark Goodman and Chris Harris

Dedication

This book is dedicated to America's blue-collar workers. You are the builders and backbone of everything that makes life habitable. You provide our great nation with the essential services and skilled labor that keep our society functioning and modern civilization possible. Without the blue-collar workforce, our homes, businesses, transportation systems, infrastructure, and national security would erode. We don't know what we would do without you—and hope to never find out. Thank you for your strong work ethic, dedication, adaptability, and resilience—you are the unsung heroes of American society and have our gratitude.

—*Mark Goodman and Chris Harris*

Table of Contents

Foreword

A few months ago, Chris broached the idea of writing a book focusing solely on bridging the critical skills gap in the United States. Given my family's 45-year history of delivering technology and curriculum focused on closing this gap, my interest was piqued.

Mark Goodman and I have known each other for 17 years. He has spent his professional career delivering vital workforce development and skilled trades solutions. We first worked together as he developed an advanced wind technology training program in Idaho. Mark is a subject-matter expert in skills development, technical knowledge, and instructional design, and, more importantly, a good friend.

Professional training has been a key component of Chris Harris's success. We first connected as competitors in advanced manufacturing sales over 10 years ago, which led to a mutual respect and friendship. Chris is an exceptionally fast learner who has mastered the complexities of working with the Department of Defense, a specialty he has successfully navigated for the past 25 years as a private contractor. One of his passions is to help reduce the threat to our national security, which requires a proactive and strategic approach to tackling our nation's skills gap problem.

Mark and Chris have spent the last few decades focused on training, which has helped solve workforce development, human capital, and skills-gap problems across multiple defense and industry sectors. This book is a valuable resource for anyone seeking insight into how our nation's workforce has declined to its current shortage.

Mark and Chris have outlined the specific skills missing from education, industry, and the Department of Defense. Most importantly, viable solutions and strategies for correcting these critical problems are presented concisely. By gaining a deeper understanding of the skills gap and the collaborative efforts needed to address it, we can take necessary steps toward rebuilding the solid foundation that ensures the security, stability, and prosperity of our great nation.

Warner Brown / CEO of Tech-Labs and X-Cal

Introduction

T he skills gap in America is a genuine and pressing problem. At no other time in our history have we found ourselves in a state of severely diminished industrial and manufacturing capacity. Our nation is currently facing a shortage of qualified workers. This has caused multiple problems, including reduced productivity and millions of unfilled jobs, as well as hindering our ability to expand technological innovation. All businesses, regardless of size, sector, or industry, struggle to produce goods and services because of a lack of a skilled workforce.

So, how did we get here? We have spent the better part of the last four generations teaching our children the value of education and the importance of acquiring knowledge so that high-paying, white-collar job opportunities would be within their reach. Meanwhile, the older generations continued to use the knowledge they had gained through lifetimes of experience to keep manufacturing moving forward. No single industry, technology, or set of core competencies is exempt. They are all suffering. We find ourselves in a position where workers with the required sets of skills are retiring at an alarming rate. To make matters worse, there are not enough people with the capabilities to replace them.

Having spent the last forty years working directly in the manufacturing industry, I have gained firsthand experience with the workforce development issues the United States is facing. I have collaborated with many of the world's largest organizations, understanding the broad-based and specific issues that are causing them to perform at levels far below their potential.

I began my career in the electric motor industry and learned firsthand what it takes to keep products flowing through the factory doors—every day and on time. As adult learning became one of my life's passions, I pursued a BS degree in Instructional Design with a focus on organizational development across all areas of the skilled trades. Following college, I worked in education, helping design a federally accredited college technical program and spending years teaching a variety of courses designed to prepare students for careers in industrial occupations.

As the Lean Movement infiltrated all areas of manufacturing, I studied Lean Six Sigma, advancing through the ranks to earn my Black Belt certification. I've spent years providing skill gap analysis and training development consultations for major industrial organizations with worldwide operations. I have designed training initiatives in the United States, Africa, and the Middle East and painstakingly drafted state-approved workforce apprenticeship programs.

For years, when people ask me what I do for a living, I like to say, "My work spans from pickles to space rockets—and everything in between." I have witnessed some of the most remarkable processes within the food and beverage, mining, textile, defense, automotive, steel, distribution, pharmaceutical, and technology industries at countless locations around the globe. Today, I'm fortunate to get to work with one of the world's leading producers of interactive, cloud-based learning solutions for workforce development and manufacturers of hands-on technical learning systems. I'm proud to help support them on their journey to transform the global workforce—one life at a time.

I am pleased to co-author this book with my colleague and good friend, Mr. Chris Harris. Chris has an impressive professional background, particularly in his 25 years of working with top leaders within the Department of Defense. Together, Chris and I will help you gain a deeper understanding of the workforce development problem, including its history, significance, current state, future implications, and, most importantly, a pathway to solutions. In the following chapters, Chris and I will share factual data related to the American skills gap, as well as effective strategies to help put our great nation on a vital course correction.

—*Mark Goodman / Co-Author*

Section I: 5 Skills Gap Indicators

Chapter One

Global Economy and Perspectives

A s we step deeper into the 21st century, the global economy is undergoing a seismic transformation—one that is reshaping work and the workforce. From the rise of artificial intelligence to the effects of globalization, demographic shifts, and climate change, a complex set of forces is redefining what jobs will look like and the skills needed to thrive. Understanding these changes is key for policymakers, businesses, educators, and workers alike as they prepare for an uncertain but opportunity-rich future.

A New Economic Landscape

The global economy is becoming increasingly interconnected and digital. While international trade continues to be a powerful driver of growth, geopolitical tensions, supply chain disruptions, and a growing emphasis on national resilience are prompting countries and companies to rethink their economic strategies. Digital platforms and technologies have lowered barriers to entry for businesses and freelancers worldwide, enabling more people to take part in the global economy than ever before.

Emerging economies, especially in Asia and Africa, are experiencing rapid population growth and expanding middle classes, contributing to global demand and labor supply. Meanwhile, advanced economies face slower growth, aging populations, and greater pressure to innovate and adapt to remain competitive.

Key Trends Shaping the Future Workforce

1. Automation and Artificial Intelligence (AI):
AI, robotics, and machine learning are automating routine tasks across in-

dustries, from manufacturing to finance to healthcare. While this threatens to displace some jobs, it also creates demands for new roles in tech development, data analysis, and human-centered fields such as customer experience and creative work. The future workforce will need to embrace lifelong learning and adaptability to stay relevant in an AI-enhanced world.

2. The Rise of Remote and Hybrid Work:
The COVID-19 pandemic accelerated a global shift toward remote work, and many of those changes are here to stay. Hybrid work models are now common, especially in knowledge-based industries. This has global implications, as companies tap into a broader, borderless talent pool while workers seek flexibility and work-life balance. However, this also brings challenges in terms of digital infrastructure and workplace culture.

3. Skills Over Degrees:
Employers are increasingly prioritizing skills over formal education credentials. With the rapid pace of change, traditional degrees often cannot keep up with evolving job requirements. Short-term certifications, bootcamps, and online learning platforms are gaining popularity, offering faster, more flexible paths to employment. Soft skills—such as communication, critical thinking, and emotional intelligence—are becoming just as valuable as technical expertise.

4. Demographic Shifts:
Aging populations in developed nations and youth surges in developing countries will create contrasting workforce challenges. Proactive and informed employment strategies are critical to harnessing the full potential of global talent. Companies that prioritize searching for quality talent before it is needed will be better positioned to innovate and compete in a global marketplace.

Perspectives on Preparing for the Future

Governments, businesses, and educational institutions all play a role in preparing the future workforce. Investments in digital infrastructure, reskilling programs, and universal access to quality education will be essential. Cross-sector partnerships can help align training with labor market needs and ensure fair access to emerging opportunities.

Companies, for their part, must become agile learning organizations—building internal capabilities, fostering adaptability, and supporting employee growth. Human resource strategies must shift from static job roles to dynamic skill portfolios.

Meanwhile, individuals will need to take greater ownership of their career paths. Self-directed learning, adaptability, and resilience will be the cornerstones of professional success. The mindset of "learn once, work forever" is being replaced with "learn always, evolve constantly."

Conclusion

Forces that are both global and deeply personal will shape the future workforce. While the pace of change may feel overwhelming, it also brings new opportunities to create a more inclusive, innovative, and resilient world of work. Navigating this future requires a commitment to collaboration, continuous learning, and a willingness to reimagine what it means to work and thrive in a global economy.

Chapter Two

U.S. Workforce Development

Workforce development in the United States has become a central topic in national discussions about economic competitiveness and innovation. As industries evolve and the demand for skilled labor grows more complex, the U.S. must rethink how it prepares individuals for careers that match the needs of the 21st-century economy. Workforce development is more than just job training—it's a strategic investment in people that fuels productivity, supports economic growth, and creates resilient communities.

What Is Workforce Development?

Workforce development refers to the broad range of policies, programs, and initiatives designed to equip workers with the skills, knowledge, and support they need to succeed in the labor market. This includes everything from K-12 education alignment, technical training, apprenticeships, and adult education to career counseling, employer partnerships, and reskilling programs for displaced workers.

Unlike traditional education systems, employers and regional labor markets often tightly integrate workforce development with their specific needs. It aims to close the gap between what workers know and what employers require, providing practical pathways to employment and upward mobility.

Why It Matters Now?

The U.S. labor market is undergoing a profound transformation. Technology, automation, and globalization have redefined jobs across virtually every employment sector. At the same time, demographic shifts—including the retirement of baby boomers—are changing the makeup of talent pools. The COVID-19 pandemic further accelerated changes in where and how people work, revealing both strengths and shortcomings in the existing workforce system.

One of the most pressing challenges is the skills gap—where employers struggle to fill high-demand roles while many Americans remain underemployed or unemployed. Sectors such as healthcare, advanced manufacturing, IT, and skilled trades consistently report shortages of qualified workers. The disconnect highlights the need for a more responsive and inclusive workforce development system.

Key Components of Modern Workforce Development

1. Industry Partnerships:
Successful workforce initiatives increasingly involve collaboration between employers, educators, and workforce agencies. Industry-driven partnerships align training programs with real-time labor market needs, ensuring students are prepared for in-demand roles. Many regional efforts, such as sector-based strategies, bring together multiple stakeholders to target specific industries like clean energy or logistics.

2. Apprenticeships and Work-Based Learning:
Apprenticeship programs are gaining renewed interest as a proven model for workforce development. Combining classroom instruction with paid, on-the-job training, these programs offer a clear path to employment and upward mobility without requiring a four-year degree. Employers benefit from building a talent pipeline, while participants gain valuable experience and credentials.

3. Reskilling and Lifelong Learning:
As job roles evolve, workers need to update their skills continuously. Reskilling and upskilling programs help individuals transition into new roles or advance in their careers. Community colleges, online platforms, and both for-profit and nonprofit organizations are playing an increasing role in delivering flexible, affordable training for adults.

Federal and State Initiatives

Federal support for workforce development comes through programs like the Workforce Innovation and Opportunity Act (WIOA), which funds job training and career services nationwide. Recent legislation, including the CHIPS and Science Act and the Infrastructure Investment and Jobs Act, also allocates funding for workforce initiatives tied to infrastructure, clean energy, and technology.

At the state and local level, customized programs are emerging to meet regional economic needs. States are investing in technical education, apprenticeships, and workforce boards that connect employers with talent pipelines.

Conclusion

The future of U.S. workforce development lies in adaptability and collaboration. As technology continues to change the nature of work, a strong workforce development system will be essential to ensure workers aren't left behind and that American businesses remain competitive in a global economy. By aligning education with industry, investing in lifelong learning, and ensuring access for all, the U.S. can build a workforce that is resilient, diverse, and ready for the jobs of tomorrow.

Chapter Three

U.S. National Trends

In recent years, one of the most pressing challenges facing the American labor market is the widening national skills gap—the disconnect between the skills employers need and the skills workers possess. As the economy evolves, especially in the face of rapid technological advancement, this gap has emerged as a critical issue affecting businesses, workers, and the broader U.S. economy.

What Is the National Skills Gap?

The term "skills gap" refers to the mismatch between the qualifications employers are looking for and the skills that job seekers actually bring to the table. This isn't just about advanced degrees or certifications—it's also about hands-on experience, technical know-how, and soft skills like communication, critical thinking/problem-solving, and adaptability.

Key Trends Driving the Gap

1. Technological Transformation:
Automation, artificial intelligence, and other advanced technologies are transforming industries at a rapid pace. While these innovations are creating new job opportunities, they also demand new skills. Fields such as cybersecurity, data science, and software development are booming, but employers struggle to find workers with the required expertise. Meanwhile, traditional jobs are being redefined, requiring workers to upskill or risk obsolescence.

2. Decline in Vocational Training:
There has been a steady decline in vocational and technical education programs in the U.S. over the past few decades. As the push for four-year

college degrees intensified, many high schools and community colleges cut back on trade and technical training programs. This has led to a shortage of workers in skilled trades such as plumbing, welding, and electrical work—sectors that are essential and well-paying, but often overlooked.

3. Education-to-Work Mismatch:
Many recent graduates enter the job market with degrees that don't align with current labor-market needs. While higher education enrollment remains strong, not all programs equip students with marketable, in-demand skills. Employers frequently report difficulty filling positions that require mid-level technical skills, even as college graduates struggle to find jobs that match their qualifications.

4. Demographic Shifts and Retirements:
An aging workforce is contributing to the skills gap, particularly in sectors like manufacturing and construction. As baby boomers retire, they take decades of experience with them, and there's often a shortage of younger workers prepared to step into those roles. Many times, younger generations lack exposure to or interest in these industries, further widening the gap.

The Economic Impact

The skills gap carries significant economic consequences. According to data from the U.S. Chamber of Commerce and the National Federation of Independent Business, a majority of small and mid-sized businesses report difficulty finding qualified workers. Unfilled jobs lead to reduced productivity, slower growth, and increased costs for training and recruiting. On a national scale, this inefficiency can hinder innovation and weaken the country's global competitiveness.

Solutions and the Road Ahead

To address the skills gap, a multifaceted approach is essential:

- Expanding Apprenticeships and On-the-Job Training: Programs that combine work experience with classroom learning are making a comeback. Companies partnering with community colleges and workforce development organizations are seeing success in filling critical roles.

- Reinvesting in Career and Technical Education (CTE): A renewed focus on vocational education can provide pathways to high-paying, skilled careers without requiring a four-year degree.

- Upskilling and Reskilling Initiatives: Employers are investing more in training current employees to meet developing business needs. Government programs and nonprofit initiatives are also stepping in to help displaced or underemployed workers gain new skills.

- Stronger Industry-Education Collaboration: Aligning educational curricula with the needs of local industries can ensure that students graduate with job-ready skills. Early exposure to in-demand fields through internships and co-op programs can also help close the gap.

Conclusion

The U.S. skills gap is not a static issue—it reflects broader societal, economic, and technological shifts. While the challenge is complex, it also presents an opportunity: to rethink how we prepare workers for the future and how we value different education and training. By investing in people and aligning efforts across sectors, the nation can build a more adaptable and future-ready workforce.

Chapter Four

U.S. Educational Systems

A s the demands of the American labor market develop, education-al systems across the United States are playing a pivotal role in preparing the next generation of workers. No longer focused solely on academic achievement, schools, colleges, and universities are increasingly aligning their programs with workforce development goals. This shift reflects a broader recognition that education must equip students with the skills, experiences, and credentials needed to succeed in a transforming economy.

The Changing Role of Education

Traditionally, U.S. education systems have emphasized college prepara-tion and four-year degrees as the primary path to career success. While this route remains valuable, it no longer guarantees job security or economic mobility. Employers today are looking for a broader range of qualifications—including technical skills, hands-on experience, and soft skills like communication and adaptability.

In response, educational institutions are reimagining how they prepare students—not just for graduation, but for meaningful, in-demand careers. Workforce development has become a shared responsibility between K-12 schools, community colleges, universities, and industry partners.

K-12 Education: Early Exposure and Career Pathways

Across the country, K-12 school systems are introducing career explo-ration at earlier stages. Programs like Career and Technical Education (CTE) offer students hands-on learning in areas like healthcare, IT, manufacturing, and skilled trades—often leading to industry certifications or dual enrollment credits. These programs not only provide practical skills but also help students understand the real-world applications of their education.

Initiatives like career academies, internships, and job shadowing are also gaining traction, giving high school students direct exposure to the workforce. Many districts partner with local businesses and community colleges to develop career pathways that guide students from high school into postsecondary training or employment.

Community Colleges: Gateways to Opportunities

Community colleges have a long history of providing preparatory training across a wide range of core competencies, providing an important component of the workforce development efforts in the U.S. Their ties to local economies, flexible programming, and affordability uniquely position community colleges to help train students to qualify for a wide range of occupational opportunities. Many offer short-term certification programs, associate degrees, and apprenticeships tailored to meet the needs of regional industries.

In recent years, community colleges have expanded their role in reskilling and upskilling adult learners. From displaced workers to returning veterans, these institutions serve as gateways to new career opportunities. Partnerships with employers help ensure that curricula stay relevant, and many programs offer job placement services to support graduates' transition into the workforce.

Universities: Embracing Skills and Innovation

While universities have traditionally focused on academic theory and research, many are now integrating workforce development into their missions. This includes expanding access to certificate programs, offering interdisciplinary majors that reflect developing industries (like data analytics, logistics, or sustainability), and increasing opportunities for experiential learning, such as co-ops, internships, and service projects.

Some universities are also working with businesses to design custom training programs and invest in innovation hubs where students can develop entrepreneurial skills. These efforts reflect a growing understanding that even graduates with liberal arts or research degrees must be prepared to adapt in a competitive job market.

Cross-Sector Collaboration: The Key to Success

One of the most promising trends in workforce development is the rise of collaboration between educational institutions, government agencies, and industry. Public-private partnerships are helping to align education with labor market needs and create smooth transitions from school to work.

Programs like Perkins V, the reauthorization of the federal Career and Technical Education Act, emphasize industry input in curriculum design and promote data-sharing between schools and employers. Similarly, state-led initiatives such as California's Strong Workforce Program or Tennessee's Drive to 55 are leveraging education systems to close skills gaps and boost economic mobility.

Conclusion

Workforce development is no longer a peripheral concern—it's becoming central to the mission of education in the United States. As technological, economic, and societal changes continue to shape the future of work, educational institutions must remain agile. By integrating career readiness into every level of learning, from elementary school through higher education, the U.S. can ensure that its students are not only knowledgeable but job-ready. Through innovation and collaboration, America's educational systems are poised to be powerful engines for workforce transformation and long-term economic resilience.

Chapter Five

U.S. Economic Growth

T he U.S. economy, the largest in the world, has long been a pillar of global stability and innovation. Built on a foundation of entrepreneurship, technological advancement, and consumer-driven demand, the American economy continues to evolve in response to shifting domestic and global dynamics. While the nation has faced significant challenges in recent years—including a global pandemic, inflationary pressures, and geopolitical uncertainty—its economic engine remains resilient. Understanding the factors driving U.S. economic growth and those that could influence its future trajectory is key to navigating the path ahead.

Recent Economic Performance

Following the severe economic contraction caused by the COVID-19 pandemic in 2020, the U.S. economy experienced a strong rebound in 2021 and early 2022. Government stimulus programs and a surge in consumer demand fueled GDP growth and job recovery. However, this swift rebound also contributed to a new challenge—inflation.

Inflation reached its highest levels in four decades during 2022, prompting the Federal Reserve to aggressively raise interest rates in an effort to stabilize prices. These actions slowed the pace of growth through late 2022 and into 2023, with concerns over a potential recession looming. Despite these pressures, the economy remained surprisingly resilient. Strong consumer spending, steady job creation, and business investment helped keep growth in positive territory.

Key Drivers of Growth

Several core elements continue to support U.S. economic growth:

1. Consumer Spending:
Consumer expenditures account for roughly 70% of U.S. GDP. A relatively low unemployment rate, rising wages in certain sectors, and household savings accumulated during the pandemic have kept consumer activity robust, even in the face of higher interest rates.

2. Innovation and Technology:
The U.S. remains a global leader in technology and innovation, particularly in sectors like artificial intelligence, biotechnology, and clean energy. Tech hubs across the country, including Silicon Valley, Boston, and Austin, continue to attract capital, talent, and entrepreneurship, driving high-value economic activity.

3. Business Investment:
U.S. companies have steadily increased capital investments in automation, infrastructure, and research and development (R&D). Government incentives—such as those in the CHIPS and Science Act—are also encouraging domestic manufacturing and technological advancement.

4. Labor Market Strength:
While many sectors are experiencing a skills shortage, the overall labor market remains strong. Employment levels have surpassed pre-pandemic highs, and wage growth continues to outpace inflation in several industries, supporting economic momentum.

Challenges on the Horizon

Despite positive trends, several headwinds could pose risks to future U.S. economic growth:

1. Inflation and Interest Rates:
Although inflation has begun to cool, the Federal Reserve remains cautious. Higher interest rates could weigh on borrowing, investment, and consumer spending, particularly in housing and construction. The balance between controlling inflation and avoiding a sharp economic slowdown remains delicate.

2. Workforce and Skills Gap:
A mismatch between available jobs and workers' skills threatens productivity and limits business growth. Addressing this issue through education

and training will be essential for sustaining long-term economic expansion.

3. Global Uncertainty:
Geopolitical tensions, including conflicts abroad and strained trade relations, could disrupt supply chains and reduce investor confidence. As a globalized economy, the U.S. is not immune to external shocks.

4. National Debt and Fiscal Policy:
Federal deficits and mounting national debt raise questions about the long-term sustainability of government spending. Although recent infrastructure and clean energy investments aim to stimulate growth, policymakers must balance spending with fiscal responsibility.

The Outlook Ahead

Economists expect moderate U.S. economic growth over the next few years. While some economists forecast slower growth because of tight monetary policy and global uncertainties, others see strong potential in America's innovation capacity, diversified economy, and entrepreneurial spirit.

Strategic investments in infrastructure, energy independence, and workforce development are laying the groundwork for long-term competitiveness. Demographic changes, digital transformation, and developing consumer preferences will continue to shape the economic landscape.

Conclusion

The U.S. economy stands at a pivotal moment—resilient, yet facing complex challenges. By addressing structural issues like the skills gap, embracing innovation, and navigating policy choices with care, the nation has the opportunity not only to sustain growth but to lead the global economy into a new era of sustainable prosperity.

Section 2: 8 Skills Gap Causes

Chapter Six

Societal Biases and Influences

D iscussions of the U.S. skills gap often focus on education systems, economic trends, and technological change. But less frequently explored are the powerful cultural and psychological forces that shape career choices long before a person enters the workforce. Societal biases and marketing influences have played a significant, and often overlooked, role in steering people away from high-demand careers and contributing to the skills gap the country faces today.

The Prestige of the Four-Year Degree

For decades, American society has promoted a singular path to success: earning a four-year college degree. Parents, educators, the media, and policymakers have reinforced this belief, creating a cultural hierarchy that places traditional academic achievement above other forms of learning. This stigmatization of vocational and technical education often views it as a last resort instead of a preferred option.

This bias has contributed to declining enrollment in trade programs, apprenticeships, and community colleges, even as industries such as manufacturing, construction, and the skilled trades face massive labor shortages. Electricians, welders, HVAC technicians, and other tradespeople are in high demand, with aging workforces and not enough new entrants to replace them. Society often overlooks these careers because they don't fit the accepted image of "success."

Gender Stereotypes and Career Expectations

Societal biases have also created deeply entrenched ideas about which careers are "appropriate" for different genders. Messages—subtle and overt—influence children's views of themselves and their career potential from a young age. Outdated notions that STEM fields better suit boys might steer girls away from them and could discourage boys from pursuing careers in nursing, education, or caregiving, limiting the talent pool in these essential sectors.

These gendered expectations reinforce occupational segregation and prevent many individuals from pursuing fulfilling and lucrative careers simply because they don't match the stereotypical profile. This not only perpetuates inequality but also narrows the workforce pipeline in areas that are critically understaffed.

Marketing's Influence on Career Perception

Marketing and media powerfully shape perceptions of certain careers. Television shows, movies, advertisements, and social media often glamorize certain professions—like tech entrepreneurs, lawyers, doctors, and influencers—while ignoring or devaluing others. Rarely do we see realistic portrayals of tradespeople, technicians, or factory workers, despite their crucial contributions to the economy.

This skewed representation affects how young people imagine their futures. When marketing highlights only a narrow range of careers as desirable or prestigious, students may overlook high-demand fields that offer stability, growth, and good pay simply because they don't see them represented in a positive light.

Colleges and universities often market themselves as the only legitimate post-high school path, further discouraging exploration of alternatives like technical schools or apprenticeships. The constant messaging that success equals a bachelor's degree has left millions of Americans under-prepared for jobs that require unique skills.

The Consequences: A Widening Gap

These societal and marketing-driven influences created a self-reinforcing cycle: people overlook or stigmatize certain careers, leading to fewer people training for them, which then leads to shortages and an even wider skills gap. Cultural messaging that, for years, downplayed the value of these careers shaped the talent pipeline, causing employers in manufacturing, health care, logistics, and IT to consistently report difficulty hiring qualified workers for needed jobs.

Changing the Narrative

Closing the skills gap requires more than new policies or funding—it demands a cultural shift. Society must broaden its definition of success and challenge outdated narratives about education and work. This means elevating the visibility and value of skilled trades, diversifying representation in media and marketing, and actively encouraging all students—regardless of gender, background, or academic inclination—to explore a wide range of career options.

Conclusion

By confronting the cultural biases and marketing influences that shape our views on work, the U.S. can build a more inclusive, balanced, and effective workforce—one that meets the needs of the economy and honors the full spectrum of talent within its population.

Chapter Seven

Aging and Retiring Workforce

T he American workforce is undergoing a profound demographic transformation. As millions of baby boomers—those born between 1946 and 1964—reach retirement age, the U.S. faces an unprecedented wave of workforce exits that will have lasting implications for the economy, industries, and future generations of workers. The aging and retiring workforce is not just a trend; It is a structural shift that touches everything from labor shortages to knowledge transfer and productivity.

A Generation on the Brink of Retirement

According to data from the U.S. Census Bureau and the Bureau of Labor Statistics (BLS), approximately 10,000 baby boomers reach age 65 every day. By 2030, all boomers will be at least 65, and a significant portion will have exited the workforce. This demographic shift represents one of the largest retirement waves in U.S. history.

For decades, baby boomers have been the backbone of the American economy, filling roles in manufacturing, construction, education, healthcare, and leadership positions across every sector. Their impending departure leaves not only vacancies in the workforce but also a gap in institutional knowledge, experience, and mentorship.

Economic and Industry Impact

The retirement of such a large cohort of experienced workers presents several economic challenges:

1. Labor Shortages:
Key industries such as healthcare, skilled trades, and transportation are

already facing difficulty filling roles, and the exodus of older workers exacerbates the problem. Many of these roles require specialized training or licensure, and younger generations are not entering them quickly enough to keep up with demand.

2. Loss of Knowledge and Leadership:
Older workers often hold critical institutional knowledge and serve as mentors or leaders within organizations. Their departure can lead to knowledge gaps and disruptions in operations if proper succession planning and knowledge-transfer strategies are not in place.

3. Increased Demand for Healthcare Services:
Ironically, while the healthcare sector is losing experienced workers, it is also experiencing rising demand because of the aging population. This double pressure creates an urgent need for more workers in elder care, nursing, and support services—roles that are increasingly hard to fill.

4. Slower Economic Growth:
A shrinking labor force can lead to slower overall economic growth. Fewer workers means reduced productivity, lower consumer spending, and increased pressure on entitlement programs like Social Security and Medicare.

Why Younger Workers Aren't Filling the Gap Fast Enough

Several factors contribute to the slower entry of younger workers into the workforce:

- Declining Birth Rates: The U.S. birth rate has been steadily decreasing for decades, meaning there are simply fewer young people entering the labor force.

- Skills Mismatch: Many younger workers lack the training or interest in fields where labor shortages are most acute, such as skilled trades or STEM-related careers.

- Changing Work Preferences: Younger generations often prioritize work-life balance, flexibility, and purpose over job stability or long-term tenure—contrasting with the work ethos of many baby boomers.

Solutions and Strategies

We can mitigate the impact of the unavoidable demographic shift and adapt to a changing workforce by doing the following.

1. Retaining Older Workers Longer:
Many older Americans are open to working beyond traditional retirement age—especially in part-time or flexible roles. Policies that support phased retirement, remote work, or reduced hours can encourage experienced employees to stay engaged longer.

2. Investing in Workforce Development:
Training and upskilling younger workers to fill critical roles is essential. Expanding access to apprenticeships, trade programs, and STEM education can help bridge the gap.

3. Intergenerational Knowledge Transfer:
Employers can formalize mentorship programs to ensure that older workers pass on their knowledge and expertise before retiring. This helps preserve institutional memory and prepares younger employees for leadership.

4. Leveraging Technology:
Automation and AI can help offset some labor shortages, particularly in repetitive or labor-intensive tasks. However, these technologies must complement—not replace—human workers, especially in fields requiring emotional intelligence or specialized skills.

Conclusion

The aging and retiring U.S. workforce presents one of the greatest workforce challenges of the 21st century. It's not just about filling empty positions—it's about preparing for a fundamental change in how the economy operates. By planning, investing in training, and improving how we use our workforce, the U.S. can adapt to population changes and create a more flexible and prepared workforce for the future.

Chapter Eight

Declining Labor Force Participation

A round the world, countries are grappling with a critical and increasingly urgent issue: a decline in workforce participation. From industrialized nations to emerging economies, fewer people are taking part in the labor force relative to the working-age population. While the reasons behind this trend vary by region, the implications are clear and far-reaching—slower economic growth, increased strain on social systems, and challenges in sustaining innovation and productivity.

What Is Workforce Participation?

Workforce participation refers to the percentage of the working-age population (typically those aged 15–64) that is employed or actively seeking employment. A high participation rate generally signals a healthy economy with strong labor market engagement. Conversely, a declining rate indicates that large portions of the population are disengaging from work—either by choice, necessity, or systemic barriers.

The Global Picture

According to data from the International Labour Organization (ILO), global labor force participation has been steadily declining over the past two decades. In 2000, the global participation rate stood at around 66%. By 2023, that figure had dropped to below 60%. High-income countries show this downward trend most significantly; However, it also affects middle-and low-income nations differently.

Several major factors are driving this decline, and they vary across regions and demographics.

Demographic Shifts

One of the most significant contributors to the declining global workforce is population aging. In countries like Japan, Germany, South Korea, and Italy, low birth rates and rising life expectancies have created aging populations with shrinking labor pools. As more people retire and fewer young workers enter the workforce, participation rates organically fall.

China is also facing a rapidly aging population, a legacy of decades of population control policies. Once viewed as an inexhaustible source of labor, China's workforce peaked in 2015 and has been declining ever since, thus raising concerns about future productivity and economic competitiveness.

Youth Disengagement and Education

In many countries, especially developing economies, a growing number of young people are neither employed nor in education or training—often referred to as NEETs. Economic instability, lack of job opportunities, and poor alignment between education systems and labor market needs contribute to this disengagement.

Ironically, in higher-income countries, extended education is also playing a role in reducing workforce participation, at least temporarily. Young adults are staying in school longer, delaying their entry into the labor market. While education is essential, delayed participation can affect long-term economic momentum, especially when it's not aligned with job market demands.

Gender Gaps and Care Responsibilities

Gender inequality continues to play a significant role in workforce participation. In many countries, particularly in parts of South Asia, the Middle East, and North Africa, women's participation remains significantly lower than men's because of cultural, legal, and structural barriers.

Globally, women endure most caregiving responsibilities for children, the elderly, and others, frequently leading to career disruption or part-time work. Lack of affordable childcare and eldercare services further discourages full participation.

The Pandemic Effect

The COVID-19 pandemic sped up workforce disengagement across the globe. Lockdowns, business closures, and public health concerns drove millions out of the labor force—many of whom have not returned. Older workers retired earlier than expected, and others reevaluated their work-life balance, opting out of traditional employment models altogether. The rise of remote work and the gig economy has also changed how people take part in the workforce, with many working informally or outside of standard labor metrics.

Consequences of Declining Participation

A shrinking workforce poses several risks:

- Slower economic growth, as fewer people contribute to productivity.

- Increased dependency ratios, with fewer workers supporting more retirees.

- Higher government spending on healthcare, pensions, and social services.

- Talent shortages, particularly in key sectors like healthcare, technology, and the skilled trades.

Addressing the Challenge

Reversing the decline in workforce participation requires a multifaceted approach:

- Investing in education and training, especially for youth and marginalized populations.

- Encouraging older workers to stay longer through flexible and age-friendly work environments.

- Expanding childcare and caregiving support to allow more women and caregivers to take part fully.

- Reforming labor policies to make formal work more attractive and accessible.

Conclusion

The global decline in workforce participation is not a passing trend—it is a structural issue with long-term consequences. If left unaddressed, it could undermine economic progress and deepen inequality worldwide. By identifying root causes and implementing forward-thinking policies, countries can rebuild stronger, more resilient labor forces to meet the demands of the 21st-century global economy.

Chapter Nine

Disruptive Technology Advancements

I n every era, certain innovations emerge that reshape the way people live, work, and interact. Today, we are witnessing a wave of disruptive technological advancements that are not only changing industries but redefining entire economic models, social structures, and the nature of work itself. From artificial intelligence (AI) to biotechnology and blockchain, these breakthroughs are speeding up at a pace never seen before—and their effects are both transformative and unpredictable.

What Is Disruptive Technology?

Disruptive technology refers to innovations that significantly alter or replace existing products, services, or business models. Unlike incremental improvements, disruptive technologies often start by serving niche markets or underperforming compared to established solutions. However, as they develop, they rapidly outperform legacy systems, leading to widespread adoption and, eventually, the disruption of entire industries.

The classic example is the personal computer, which disrupted typewriters and mainframes, or streaming services, which overtook traditional cable TV. Today's disruptive technologies are more complex and far-reaching—affecting everything from healthcare and transportation to finance, education, and manufacturing.

Key Disruptive Technologies Transforming the World

1. Artificial Intelligence and Machine Learning:
AI is arguably the most transformative technology of our time. Machine learning algorithms can now process data, recognize patterns, and make decisions faster and more accurately than humans. AI is driving automa-

tion in manufacturing, powering virtual assistants, enhancing medical diagnostics, and transforming financial services. Generative AI tools like ChatGPT are also reshaping content creation, software development, and customer service.

2. Blockchain and Decentralized Systems:
Blockchain technology, best known for enabling cryptocurrencies like Bitcoin and Ethereum, is revolutionizing how data is stored and transactions are verified. Its decentralized nature offers greater transparency, security, and efficiency in industries such as finance, supply chain management, and digital identity verification.

3. Biotechnology and Genomics:
Advancements in gene editing, personalized medicine, and synthetic biology are changing the healthcare landscape. Tools like CRISPR allow scientists to alter DNA with precision, opening the door to curing genetic diseases, improving crop yields, and even creating synthetic organisms. These innovations carry enormous potential but also raise significant ethical and regulatory questions.

4. Renewable Energy and Battery Storage:
The push toward clean energy has sparked innovation in solar, wind, and battery technologies. Disruptive advances in energy storage are making renewable power more viable, reducing dependence on fossil fuels, and transforming the global energy infrastructure.

5. Quantum Computing:
Though still in early stages, quantum computing promises to solve problems that are currently intractable for classical computers. It could revolutionize fields like cryptography, materials science, and logistics—once the technology matures and becomes more accessible.

Economic and Workforce Impacts

Disruptive technologies offer immense benefits, but they also come with challenges—particularly for the workforce. Automation and AI, for instance, can increase productivity but may displace workers in routine or manual roles. According to a report by McKinsey, up to 30% of current jobs could be automated by 2030, with mid-skill roles being the most vulnerable.

These technologies create new industries, job categories, and demand for advanced skills. The rise of AI and data science has already generated a surge in demand for software developers, machine learning engineers, and cybersecurity experts. Lifelong learning, digital literacy, and adaptability are becoming essential traits for future workers.

Social and Ethical Considerations

With great power comes great responsibility. Disruptive technologies also raise complex ethical issues—from data privacy and surveillance to AI bias and unequal access. Policymakers, educators, and industry leaders must work collaboratively to ensure that innovation serves the public good and that the benefits are widely shared.

Looking Ahead

Disruption is no longer an occasional phenomenon—it is the new normal. Organizations and individuals must be prepared to continuously adapt to new realities. The countries and companies that thrive will be those that invest in research, embrace innovation, and build resilient systems capable of navigating constant change.

Conclusion

Disruptive technology advancements are reshaping the future at an unprecedented pace. While they bring uncertainty and challenge the status quo, they also unlock new opportunities for growth, progress, and problem-solving. By approaching them with vision and responsibility, we can harness their power to build a more dynamic and forward-looking society.

Chapter Ten

Changing Industry and Job Requirements

As technology accelerates and global markets evolve, industries across the board are transforming—and with them, the jobs they support. From automation and digitization to climate-conscious production and remote work, these shifts are forcing employers to rethink the skills and qualifications they seek. For workers, it means that job requirements are no longer static. Instead, they are dynamic, continuously adapting to meet the needs of a changing economy.

Industry Transformation and Its Impact on Work

Every major industry is experiencing disruption. In manufacturing, smart factories are using robotics and data analytics to streamline operations. In healthcare, digital tools like telemedicine and electronic health records are now the norm. The financial services sector has become increasingly automated, with artificial intelligence handling everything from fraud detection to customer service.

These changes are altering not just the jobs available, but also what those jobs demand. Roles that once required only manual labor or routine tasks now call for a blend of technical knowledge, critical thinking, and adaptability.

The Rise of Digital Skills

One of the most noticeable shifts in job requirements is the growing need for digital literacy. Across virtually every industry, proficiency with technology is no longer optional. Even traditionally low-tech roles now require familiarity with digital platforms—whether it's using a point-of-sale system in retail, inputting data in construction, or managing patient records in healthcare.

More advanced digital skills are also in high demand. Data analysis, cybersecurity, cloud computing, and software development are now essential in fields like finance, logistics, and marketing. Employers are not only looking for specialists in these areas but are increasingly valuing generalist workers who can understand and use data effectively in their everyday roles.

Soft Skills Take Center Stage

While technical skills are critical, soft skills—such as communication, teamwork, problem-solving, and adaptability—have become equally, if not more, important. As machines take over routine tasks, human-centric skills that cannot be easily automated are gaining value.

For example, in customer-facing industries like hospitality and healthcare, empathy and interpersonal communication remain irreplaceable. In remote and hybrid workplaces, collaboration tools have changed how teams interact, making strong virtual communication and time management essential.

Moreover, employers are seeking individuals who are agile learners—those who can quickly pick up new tools and adapt to shifting work environments. Lifelong learning is no longer a luxury; it's a necessity.

Credentialing and Experience: Shifting Expectations

The traditional emphasis on four-year degrees is waning in many sectors. Employers are increasingly open to alternative endorsements, such as industry certifications, online courses, boot camps, and stackable micro-credentials that demonstrate specific, job-ready skills.

Experience-based hiring is also gaining momentum. Skills-based hiring practices assess what a candidate can do, rather than just where they went to school. This shift creates new pathways to employment for non-traditional candidates, including career changers, veterans, and individuals without formal degrees.

Internships, apprenticeships, and project-based learning are also becoming valuable ways for job seekers to build practical experience and stand out in competitive job markets.

Green and Sustainable Skills

With a growing emphasis on environmental sustainability, many industries are integrating green practices into their operations. This trend is creating a demand for new skills in energy efficiency, sustainable design, waste reduction, and environmental compliance.

From renewable energy technicians to sustainability analysts, job roles are emerging to support the transition to a greener economy. Even existing roles—such as architects, engineers, and supply chain managers—are being redefined to include sustainability competencies.

Preparing for the Future

To succeed in this shifting landscape, both employers and workers must embrace a mindset of continuous growth, which includes:

- For workers, this means proactively upskilling, staying informed about industry trends, and being willing to pivot as opportunities arise.

- For employers, it means investing in employee training, embracing inclusive hiring practices, and building a culture that values adaptability.

Conclusion

As industries continue to change, so too will the jobs that power them. The future of work demands a workforce that is agile, skilled, and open to lifelong learning. Job requirements are no longer rigid checklists—they are developing frameworks that reflect a world in constant motion. By understanding and adapting to these changes, workers and employers alike can thrive in the industries of tomorrow.

Chapter Eleven

Traditional Education vs. Skills Mismatch

In today's rapidly changing job market, the gap between what traditional education provides and what employers actually need has become a growing concern. This disparity, often referred to as the "skills mismatch," highlights a pressing issue: graduates are entering the workforce without the practical, job-ready skills required to succeed in modern industries. As the pace of technological change speeds up, and the nature of work continues to shift, rethinking the role and structure of education has become more crucial than ever.

The Structure of Traditional Education

Traditional education, particularly at the university level, has long been considered the gold standard for preparing individuals for professional success. It emphasizes theoretical knowledge, critical thinking, and foundational learning. Students spend years studying subjects within a fixed curriculum, often with limited exposure to hands-on experience or real-world applications.

While this model has produced generations of thinkers, scholars, and professionals, it has also struggled to keep up with the demands of today's dynamic labor market. Many degree programs have not evolved significantly over time, resulting in a curriculum that can be outdated by the time students graduate. Moreover, the rigid structure of traditional education often lacks the flexibility needed to quickly adapt to new industries, emerging technologies, and changing skill sets.

Understanding the Skills Mismatch

The skills mismatch refers to the disconnect between the competencies that job seekers possess and the qualifications that employers are looking for. This issue manifests in two major ways: overqualification and underqualification. On one hand, many graduates cannot find jobs in their fields, or they accept roles that do not require a degree. On the other hand, employers in industries such as technology, healthcare, and advanced manufacturing report difficulty finding candidates with the right technical or soft skills.

According to reports by the World Economic Forum and various labor market studies, skills such as data analysis, digital literacy, communication, adaptability, and problem-solving are increasingly in demand. However, these are not always adequately covered in traditional degree programs. As a result, even with formal education credentials, many graduates find themselves underprepared for the realities of the job market.

Why the Gap Exists

Several factors contribute to the skills mismatch. First, the lag between educational reform and market evolution is significant. Universities often take years to revise curricula, while industries can shift within months. Second, there is often a lack of collaboration between educational institutions and industry leaders. Without regular input from employers, academic programs may fail to align with current workplace needs.

Additionally, traditional education tends to prioritize academic performance over practical experience. Internships, apprenticeships, and project-based learning are optional or limited, leaving students without the real-world exposure necessary to develop applicable skills.

Bridging the Gap

To address the skills mismatch, a multifaceted approach is needed. First, educational institutions must engage more deeply with industry stakeholders to co-create curricula that reflect current and future job requirements. This collaboration can help ensure that students are not only gaining knowledge but also developing the skills employers value most.

Second, there must be greater emphasis on experiential learning. Programs that integrate internships, co-ops, case studies, and simulation exercises can give students the opportunity to apply their knowledge in practical settings. These experiences also help build soft skills such as communication, teamwork, and problem-solving.

Third, the rise of alternative education pathways—such as bootcamps, micro-credentials, and online courses—should be embraced. These options allow learners to upskill or reskill quickly and affordably, often focusing on specific industry needs.

Conclusion

The divide between traditional education and the skills required in today's job market poses a challenge not just for job seekers, but for the economy as a whole. To prepare students for meaningful careers, we must rethink how education is delivered and measured. Bridging the skills gap will require innovation, collaboration, and a willingness to evolve—so that the future workforce is equipped not just with diplomas, but with the tools to thrive.

Chapter Twelve

Insufficient Training and Development

I n an era where innovation moves at lightning speed and industries are transformed overnight by emerging technologies, companies face a critical question: Are they investing enough in their people? For many, the answer is no. Training and development are often viewed as optional perks rather than essential strategies. Yet, failing to prioritize employee development carries significant consequences—many of which are not immediately visible but are deeply damaging in the long run.

Decreased Employee Performance and Productivity

One of the most immediate impacts of underinvesting in training is diminished employee performance. When employees are not equipped with the latest tools, techniques, or knowledge relevant to their roles, their productivity inevitably suffers. They may struggle to meet performance expectations, make more mistakes, or take longer to complete tasks—all of which hinder a company's operational efficiency.

This lack of up-to-date skills can lead to a ripple effect: reduced team performance, slower project timelines, and lower-quality output. Over time, these issues can erode a company's competitiveness in its' industry and reduce customer satisfaction.

High Employee Turnover and Low Engagement

Employees today—particularly Millennials and Gen Z—place a high value on learning and growth. They want to work for companies that invest in their future and help them develop professionally. When organizations fail to provide development opportunities, employees begin to feel undervalued and stuck. This leads to disengagement, and disengaged employees are significantly more likely to seek other employment opportunities.

High turnover is more than a morale issue; it's expensive. According to estimates from the Society for Human Resource Management (SHRM), replacing an employee can cost as much as 50% to 60% of their annual salary, factoring in recruitment, onboarding, and lost productivity. In contrast, investing in employee training often costs far less and yields long-term benefits, including higher loyalty and performance.

Stalled Innovation and Growth

Training and development fuel innovation. Employees who are continuously learning bring fresh ideas, identify more efficient ways to do things, and are more adaptable to change. Without a strong learning culture, companies risk stagnation. They may continue relying on outdated processes and fail to keep up with competitors who are more agile and forward-thinking.

Moreover, companies that don't foster continuous learning often struggle to promote from within. This limits leadership development and creates gaps in the talent pipeline. In the absence of strong internal candidates, businesses may be forced to look outside for leadership—an expensive and risky strategy that can disrupt team dynamics.

Increased Risks and Compliance Issues

In industries where regulations are strict—such as finance, healthcare, and manufacturing—training isn't just a value-add; It's a necessity. Without regular development in compliance protocols, safety standards, and regulatory changes, companies expose themselves to legal and financial risks. A single compliance failure can result in hefty fines, lawsuits, or reputational damage that's difficult to repair.

Beyond compliance, untrained employees may also create cybersecurity vulnerabilities, mishandle customer data, or make costly operational errors. In this sense, training isn't just about growth—it's about risk management and business continuity.

Customer Dissatisfaction

Employees are the face of a company. Whether they work in sales, customer service, technical support, or operations, their ability to interact effectively with customers is shaped by how well they've been trained. Poorly trained staff can lead to subpar customer experiences, lost sales, and damage to the company's reputation.

In contrast, companies that prioritize training typically see better customer outcomes—because their employees are confident, competent, and capable of solving problems quickly and effectively.

Conclusion

The impact of not prioritizing training and development is both internal and external. It affects everything from productivity and employee morale to customer satisfaction and brand reputation. While training programs require time and resources, the return on investment is substantial. Companies that invest in their people build stronger teams, innovate faster, and adapt more easily to change. Ultimately, in today's knowledge-driven economy, a company's most valuable asset is its people. Organizations that recognize this and make continuous learning a strategic priority are far more likely to succeed—not just today, but in the future.

Chapter Thirteen

Soft Skills and Digital Literacy Gaps

The U.S. labor market is undergoing a seismic shift. As the economy becomes more digital, interconnected, and fast-paced, the skills that workers need to thrive are evolving. While much attention is paid to technical and specialized knowledge, two key areas often get overlooked: soft skills and digital literacy. Despite being essential in nearly every profession, both remain significant gaps across the American workforce, threatening productivity, employability, and economic competitiveness.

The Critical Role of Soft Skills

Soft skills—such as communication, collaboration, critical thinking, adaptability, and emotional intelligence—are the human-centered capabilities that allow individuals to navigate the workplace effectively. They're not tied to a specific industry or tool, but they're crucial in every role, from entry-level customer service to senior management.

Employers consistently rank soft skills among their top hiring priorities. According to surveys by LinkedIn and the National Association of Colleges and Employers (NACE), qualities like teamwork, problem-solving, and communication often outweigh hard skills for hiring and promotion decisions. Yet, many workers, especially younger generations entering the workforce, are not adequately prepared in these areas.

This soft skills gap is partly a result of how education and training systems are structured. Academic programs tend to prioritize test scores and technical content, with limited emphasis on interpersonal development. Meanwhile, remote learning and digital interactions—especially in the wake of the COVID-19 pandemic—have reduced opportunities for face-to-face communication and real-time collaboration, further weakening these crucial competencies.

The Rising Need for Digital Literacy

On the other end of the spectrum lies digital literacy—the ability to effectively use digital tools, platforms, and technologies to perform tasks, solve problems, and communicate. In today's workforce, digital literacy goes beyond basic computer skills. It includes navigating cloud-based tools, managing data, understanding cybersecurity basics, and being able to adapt to new software environments quickly.

Unfortunately, large segments of the U.S. population still lack these skills. A 2021 report from the National Skills Coalition found that one in three U.S. workers had limited or no digital skills. These gaps are particularly pronounced among older workers, low-income populations, and those without access to high-quality education or broadband infrastructure.

In a world where digital platforms dominate everything from sales and marketing to project management and customer service, digital literacy is no longer optional. Workers without these competencies face increasing barriers to employment, promotion, and long-term job security.

The Economic and Business Implications

The combined gap in soft skills and digital literacy has far-reaching consequences. For individuals, it can mean fewer job opportunities, lower wages, and limited career advancement. For employers, it can cause lower productivity, communication breakdowns, and difficulties implementing new technologies.

At a national level, these skill shortages affect the economy's ability to innovate and grow. As industries like healthcare, manufacturing, finance, and education digitize their operations, a digitally fluent and socially competent workforce becomes essential to maintain global competitiveness.

Moreover, these gaps can widen inequality. Workers who already face systemic barriers—such as those from underserved communities—may be disproportionately affected, deepening the economic divide.

Solutions: Building a Future–Ready Workforce

Addressing the soft skills and digital literacy gap requires a coordinated effort across education, business, and government.

- Educational reform is key. Schools, colleges, and training programs need to embed soft skills development and digital literacy into their core curriculum—not as electives, but as foundational competencies.

- Workplace training should be ongoing, not just a one-time onboarding process. Employers must invest in upskilling and reskilling programs that combine technical training with leadership and communication development.

- Public-private partnerships can help scale digital access, especially in rural or disadvantaged areas. Investments in broadband infrastructure and community training centers can empower more Americans to become digitally proficient.

Conclusion

The future of work is already here—and it demands more than just technical know-how. Soft skills and digital literacy are the glue that holds modern teams, technologies, and strategies together. Closing these gaps isn't just about personal development—it's about national progress. Companies, educators, and policymakers must work together to ensure that every American has the tools to thrive in the digital age.

Section 3: 12 Critical Focus Points

Chapter Fourteen

Business and Finance

The business and finance sector has long served as the backbone of the global economy, providing the capital, strategies, and infrastructure that drive growth across all sectors. From large investment banks to local credit unions, from global corporations to tech startups, this industry touches every facet of modern life. But as the world evolves—economically, technologically, and socially—so do the challenges facing this critical sector. Today, the business and finance industry finds itself at a crossroads, navigating a complex landscape filled with uncertainty and transformation.

Digital Disruption and Technological Innovation

Technology is changing the game in business and finance. AI-powered trading algorithms, robo-advisors, blockchain-based payments, and digital currencies are changing how financial services are delivered and consumed.

While these technologies offer improved efficiency, reduced costs, and enhanced customer experiences, they also present the following challenges:

- Cybersecurity threats have escalated, with financial institutions being prime targets for sophisticated attacks.

- Legacy systems in traditional banks often struggle to keep up with the agility of FinTech startups, forcing difficult and costly overhauls.

- Regulation has lagged behind innovation, creating legal uncertainties around emerging tools like cryptocurrencies and decentralized finance (DeFi).

Staying competitive now means not only adopting new technologies but doing so securely, ethically, and in compliance with evolving laws.

Regulatory Complexity and Compliance

The business and finance industry is one of the most heavily regulated sectors in the world—and for good reason. Financial crises, such as the 2008 meltdown, have shown the devastating impact of unregulated or poorly managed financial systems.

However, keeping up with constantly changing regulatory requirements—whether related to capital requirements, consumer protection, or environmental, social, and governance (ESG) disclosures—can be a significant burden. Smaller firms often lack the resources to maintain compliance teams, while global institutions must navigate multiple regulatory regimes across borders.

As financial products become more complex, transparency and consumer understanding become critical concerns, driving further regulatory scrutiny.

Economic Volatility and Market Uncertainty

Inflation, interest rate hikes, geopolitical tensions, and pandemic recovery efforts have created an era of economic uncertainty. For the finance sector, these fluctuations impact everything from lending and investing to risk management and consumer behavior.

For example:

- Rising interest rates may curb consumer borrowing and home buying.

- Volatile markets can undermine investor confidence and disrupt financial planning.

- Global supply chain disruptions affect corporate earnings and credit risk assessments.

Finance professionals must now operate in an environment where rapid change is the norm and long-term predictions are increasingly difficult.

Changing Workforce Dynamics

The industry is also facing talent challenges. Younger workers are looking for more than just a paycheck—they want purpose, flexibility, and work-life balance. Traditional corporate structures and long hours typical in finance may not appeal to the emerging workforce.

Meanwhile, there is growing demand for new skills—especially in areas like data analytics, AI, cybersecurity, and ESG investing. Reskilling existing workers and attracting top talent in these fields is now a top priority for many firms.

Sustainability and Ethical Expectations

Stakeholders—from investors to customers—are placing more emphasis on corporate responsibility and sustainability. ESG (Environmental, Social, and Governance) factors are becoming central to business and investment decisions.

However, measuring and reporting ESG performance remains inconsistent and complex. Accusations of "greenwashing" (misleading claims about sustainability) are on the rise, prompting calls for greater accountability and transparency.

Firms must now balance profitability with purpose, incorporating ethical practices into their business models without compromising performance.

Conclusion

The business and finance industry is amid a profound transformation. While it continues to play a vital role in the global economy, it must confront a wide range of challenges—from digital disruption and economic volatility to regulatory shifts and evolving societal expectations. To thrive in this new era, financial institutions and business leaders must be agile, innovative, and forward-thinking. Embracing change, investing in people and technology, and maintaining public trust will be essential not only to navigate today's challenges but to build a resilient and inclusive financial system for the future.

Chapter Fifteen

Construction

The construction industry is a vital pillar of the global economy, responsible for building the homes we live in, the roads we drive on, the schools we learn in, and the hospitals we rely on. In the United States alone, the construction sector contributes over $1.9 trillion annually to the economy and employs millions of workers. However, despite its importance, a growing list of challenges is reshaping how the industry plans, executes, and sustains construction projects.

From labor shortages and rising material costs to technological disruption and regulatory complexities, the construction industry must navigate a complex landscape to meet rising demand and modern expectations.

Labor Shortages and Skills Gaps

One of the most pressing issues in the construction sector is the persistent shortage of skilled labor. As older, experienced workers retire, there simply aren't enough younger workers entering the field to replace them. According to Associated Builders and Contractors (ABC), the U.S. construction industry needs to hire over half a million workers annually to meet current demand.

Part of the challenge stems from societal perceptions. For decades, vocational trades have been undervalued compared to four-year college degrees, leading to a decline in enrollment in trade schools and apprenticeships. As a result, contractors struggle to find qualified carpenters, electricians, plumbers, and heavy equipment operators—slowing project timelines and increasing labor costs.

Rising Material Costs and Supply Chain Disruptions

The global supply chain disruptions that began during the COVID-19 pandemic continue to affect the construction industry. Prices for materials such as lumber, steel, concrete, and copper have experienced significant volatility, making it difficult for builders to estimate costs and maintain budgets.

Additionally, delays in the delivery of key components—like windows, HVAC systems, or fixtures—can halt construction progress altogether. These disruptions not only raise costs but can jeopardize project deadlines, contract fulfillment, and client relationships.

Technological Lag and the Push for Innovation

While industries like manufacturing and finance have rapidly embraced digital transformation, construction has been slower to adopt new technologies. Many firms still rely on outdated processes, manual documentation, and siloed communication systems.

However, this is changing. Technologies such as Building Information Modeling (BIM), drones, 3D printing, augmented reality (AR), and project management software are gaining traction. These tools offer increased efficiency, better project visibility, and enhanced safety—but the transition requires investment, training, and cultural shifts that can be difficult for traditional firms to implement quickly.

Sustainability and Environmental Regulations

As climate concerns rise, the construction industry is under increasing pressure to adopt more sustainable building practices. Governments and developers alike are demanding green buildings that reduce energy consumption, lower emissions, and minimize environmental impact.

Meeting these expectations requires changes in materials, design, and construction methods. It also brings new regulatory hurdles, certifications like Leadership in Energy and Environmental Design (LEED), and added costs that some companies struggle to absorb. Despite these challenges, the push for sustainable construction is expected to grow, especially as urban populations expand and infrastructure investment increases.

Health, Safety, and Workforce Wellbeing

Construction remains one of the most dangerous industries, with high rates of injury and fatality. Ensuring worker safety is not just a regulatory requirement—it's a moral and operational imperative. Companies must invest in proper training, safety gear, and risk assessment protocols to protect their teams.

The industry is also grappling with how to better support worker wellbeing. Long hours, physically demanding labor, and high-stress environments can lead to mental health issues, burnout, and high turnover. Addressing these concerns is key to keeping talent and building a more resilient workforce.

Conclusion

The construction industry is at a critical juncture. Demand for new buildings, infrastructure, and sustainable development is surging, yet the sector faces many hurdles that threaten its ability to deliver. Labor shortages, cost pressures, technological lag, and rising environmental expectations are forcing construction leaders to rethink how they operate. By investing in workforce development, embracing innovation, and committing to sustainable practices, the industry can not only overcome these challenges but emerge stronger and more future-ready. The path forward requires collaboration, adaptability, and a willingness to build not just structures—but better systems for the future of construction.

Chapter Sixteen

Defense

The global defense industry plays a critical role in national security, technological innovation, and economic activity. In the United States alone, the defense sector supports over 3 million jobs and receives hundreds of billions in federal contracts annually. But while the industry continues to be a cornerstone of national strength, it faces a host of complex challenges in the coming years and beyond—ranging from technological disruption and geopolitical tensions to supply chain vulnerabilities and workforce shortages.

As global threats develop, the defense industry must adapt to maintain readiness, agility, and superiority.

Evolving Global Threats and Strategic Competition

One of the most significant challenges facing the defense industry is the rapid shift in global security dynamics. The return of great power competition—particularly between the U.S., China, and Russia—has redefined national defense priorities. Traditional military threats are now accompanied by asymmetric tactics, including cyberattacks, misinformation campaigns, and space-based warfare.

This means that defense contractors and military strategists must prepare for a wider range of scenarios. From hypersonic missile defense and AI-enabled warfare to space command and quantum computing, the scope of preparedness has expanded dramatically. Rapid technological advancement by rival nations only increases pressure on the defense sector to innovate at an unprecedented speed.

Modernization and Technological Integration

The pace of technological change poses a unique challenge. Defense platforms—such as fighter jets, naval ships, and missile systems—are traditionally developed over decades. But with the rapid emergence of disruptive technologies like artificial intelligence (AI), machine learning, autonomous systems, and cyber warfare tools, long development cycles can quickly render capabilities obsolete.

To stay ahead, the defense industry must embrace digital modernization, integrating new technologies into both legacy systems and next-generation platforms. This requires not only massive R&D investment but also greater collaboration with agile tech companies—many of which are unaccustomed to the complexities of defense contracting and federal procurement processes.

Supply Chain and Manufacturing Constraints

The COVID-19 pandemic and subsequent geopolitical conflicts revealed significant vulnerabilities in global supply chains, including those essential to defense. Critical components such as microchips, rare earth minerals, and aerospace parts are often sourced from a limited number of suppliers—some of whom are in adversarial or unstable regions.

This overreliance on global supply networks raises serious concerns about national security and operational readiness. To mitigate risk, the Department of Defense is pushing for supply chain resilience through domestic sourcing, nearshoring, and diversification of suppliers. However, rebuilding and re-shoring defense manufacturing capabilities will take time, resources, and sustained policy support.

Budget Constraints and Procurement Challenges

While the U.S. defense budget remains among the largest in the world, competing domestic priorities—including healthcare, education, and infrastructure—continue to apply pressure on military spending. Defense contractors must deliver more advanced capabilities within tighter budget constraints.

Additionally, the federal procurement process is notoriously complex and slow, which can stifle innovation and discourage smaller firms from participating. Simplifying acquisition policies, accelerating decision-making, and fostering public-private partnerships will be essential to improving efficiency and innovation in the defense ecosystem.

Workforce Shortages and Skills Gaps

Like many other industries, the defense sector is facing a growing shortage of skilled labor. Engineers, technicians, cybersecurity experts, and advanced manufacturing professionals are in high demand—but hard to find. At the same time, the aging workforce within traditional defense manufacturing creates risks of knowledge loss and decreased productivity.

To address this, defense firms must invest in workforce development, including partnerships with universities, apprenticeships, and reskilling programs. Cultivating interest in national security careers among younger generations—who may be more drawn to private tech firms—is also critical to sustaining long-term talent pipelines.

Conclusion

The defense industry is at a pivotal moment. As the global security environment grows more unpredictable and technologically complex, the challenges it faces are both urgent and multifaceted. From modernizing outdated systems and securing vulnerable supply chains to navigating budget constraints and building a skilled workforce, the path forward requires innovation, agility, and strategic foresight. By embracing change and fostering collaboration between government, industry, and academia, the defense sector can remain resilient and effective, ensuring that national security keeps pace with the demands of a rapidly evolving world.

Chapter Seventeen

Energy

The energy sector sits at the heart of the global economy, fueling everything from transportation and manufacturing to homes and digital infrastructure. Currently, the energy sector is navigating one of the most complex and consequential transitions in its history. With rising demand, shifting policies, environmental pressures, and geopolitical tensions, the industry is facing a series of critical challenges that will shape not only its future—but the future of the planet.

Balancing Energy Transition with Demand Growth

Perhaps the most defining challenge of the modern energy industry is managing the shift from fossil fuels to cleaner, more sustainable sources—without compromising energy availability or affordability. As countries strive to meet climate targets, reduce greenhouse gas emissions, and align with the goals of the Paris Agreement, investment in renewables like wind, solar, and hydroelectric power is surging.

However, global energy demand continues to rise—particularly in developing nations. Balancing the need for reliable, affordable power with the urgency of decarbonization is a delicate act. Renewable sources, while crucial, still face limitations related to storage, intermittency, and grid integration. Until energy storage technologies like batteries or green hydrogen scale up, fossil fuels remain a major part of the global energy mix.

Grid Reliability and Infrastructure Modernization

Aging and outdated infrastructure poses a serious risk to energy security. In many countries, including the United States, the power grid was built decades ago and is increasingly vulnerable to extreme weather events, cyberattacks, and the rising demand from electric vehicles and digital technologies.

To accommodate the rise of decentralized, renewable energy sources and ensure stable power delivery, grids must be modernized. This includes updating transmission lines, integrating smart grid technologies, and deploying real-time monitoring systems. These upgrades require massive investment and coordination among utilities, governments, and private sector players—challenges that are as logistical as they are financial.

Geopolitical Instability and Energy Security

Geopolitical tensions continue to complicate global energy markets. Conflicts in energy-rich regions, such as the Middle East and Eastern Europe, can quickly disrupt supply chains and spike prices. The war in Ukraine, for example, significantly affected the flow of natural gas to Europe and highlighted the vulnerabilities of depending on foreign sources for critical energy supplies.

In response, many nations are seeking to diversify their energy sources and boost domestic production of oil, gas, and renewables. But reshaping global energy trade and reducing dependence on volatile regions is a long-term endeavor with significant economic and political implications.

Investment and Market Uncertainty

The rapid evolution of the energy landscape has created uncertainty for investors. While there is strong interest in clean energy, inconsistent government policies, regulatory frameworks, and shifting consumer behavior can make long-term planning difficult.

Traditional oil and gas companies, in particular, face a dual challenge: maintaining profitable operations in the present while investing heavily in low-carbon alternatives. This transition requires not only financial resources but also a logical strategy and public trust—both of which are still developing.

Additionally, energy companies must respond to growing calls for Environmental, Social, and Governance (ESG) accountability. Stakeholders now expect transparency on emissions and community impact, pushing firms to report and adapt their business practices in new ways.

Workforce Transition and Skills Gaps

The transition to a cleaner energy future is creating new job opportunities, but also displacing traditional roles. The sector needs more engineers, data analysts, grid specialists, and renewable energy technicians—but struggles to find talent with the right skills.

At the same time, workers from legacy energy sectors, such as coal or oil drilling, may lack clear pathways into emerging roles. Addressing this challenge requires investment in retraining and workforce development, alongside policies that support a just transition for affected communities.

Conclusion

The energy industry is at a turning point—tasked with powering a growing world while navigating environmental limits, technological disruption, and shifting global dynamics. These challenges are immense, but so are the opportunities. By investing in innovation, building resilient infrastructure, and embracing sustainability, the energy sector can lead the way toward a more secure and low-carbon future. In a time of rapid change, one thing is clear: the energy choices made today will shape the world of tomorrow.

Chapter Eighteen

Food and Beverage

The food and beverage industry is one of the most vital sectors of the global economy, providing essential nourishment to billions while driving significant employment, trade, and innovation. In the United States alone, the industry contributes over $1.4 trillion annually to the economy and employs over 17 million people across farming, manufacturing, retail, and food service. However, this essential industry is facing an unprecedented array of challenges that are reshaping how food is grown, processed, distributed, and consumed.

From supply chain disruptions and rising costs to changing consumer preferences and climate change, the food and beverage sector must adapt to survive and thrive in a rapidly changing landscape.

Supply Chain Disruptions

One of the most persistent challenges for the food and beverage industry in recent years has been supply chain volatility. The COVID-19 pandemic exposed major weaknesses in global supply networks, and the effects continue to ripple through the system. Labor shortages, port delays, transportation bottlenecks, and geopolitical instability have all contributed to disruptions in the flow of ingredients, packaging, and finished products.

For producers, this has meant difficulty sourcing raw materials and ingredients in a timely and cost-effective way. For consumers, it has led to empty shelves, rising prices, and inconsistent product availability. Building more resilient, localized, and flexible supply chains is now a top priority for many companies.

Rising Costs and Inflation

The cost of doing business in the food and beverage sector has surged. Prices for raw ingredients such as wheat, corn, and dairy have fluctuated significantly, often driven by global market instability, climate-related crop failures, and trade tensions. At the same time, labor costs, energy prices, and transportation expenses have all increased.

These rising input costs often get passed along to consumers in the form of higher food prices—contributing to broader inflation and changing buying behaviors. For businesses, managing margins while maintaining quality and affordability is a delicate balancing act.

Labor Shortages and Workforce Challenges

From farmworkers and truck drivers to restaurant staff and food manufacturing employees, labor shortages are affecting every link in the food chain. The pandemic sped up retirements and career changes, while concerns over working conditions in agriculture and food service have made recruitment and retention more difficult.

In addition, the industry is seeing a growing need for new skill sets. As automation, e-commerce, and data analytics play a larger role in operations, the demand for tech-savvy workers is increasing. Workforce development, training, and fair labor practices will be critical to meeting future staffing needs.

Changing Consumer Preferences

Today's consumers are more health-conscious, environmentally aware, and socially responsible than ever before. They want transparency about where their food comes from, how it's made, and what impact it has on the environment and their health. As a result, demand for plant-based foods, organic products, sustainable packaging, and ethical sourcing is rising.

Food and beverage companies are under pressure to reformulate products, adopt sustainable practices, and clearly communicate their values. Those who fail to meet these expectations risk losing market share to more agile and purpose-driven competitors.

Climate Change and Environmental Pressures

The food and beverage industry is both affected by and a contributor to climate change. Droughts, floods, heatwaves, and shifting weather patterns are disrupting agricultural production, threatening food security, and increasing costs. Meanwhile, the industry itself is responsible for a significant share of greenhouse gas emissions, water use, and waste generation.

Sustainability is no longer optional. From regenerative agriculture and carbon-neutral supply chains to circular packaging and waste reduction, the industry must take bold steps to reduce its environmental footprint while continuing to feed a growing global population.

Conclusion

The food and beverage industry stands at a critical crossroads. Its challenges are complex, interconnected, and global in scope—but so are the opportunities for innovation and transformation. By investing in sustainable practices, embracing technology, and staying attuned to growing consumer needs, the industry can build a more resilient and future-ready food system. In a world facing rapid change and increasing uncertainty, the mission of the food and beverage industry remains constant: to nourish people and communities. Meeting that mission now requires not just efficiency and scale, but adaptability, responsibility, and purpose.

Chapter Nineteen

Healthcare

The healthcare industry is one of the most essential and complex sectors in the world. It touches every individual, influences public policy, drives innovation, and represents a significant portion of global economic activity. In the United States alone, healthcare spending accounts for nearly 20% of GDP. Despite its importance, the industry faces an array of challenges—from workforce shortages and rising costs to regulatory hurdles and technological disruption.

In a post-pandemic world, the spotlight on healthcare has never been brighter—and the urgency to address these challenges has never been greater.

Workforce Shortages and Burnout

One of the most immediate and pressing issues in healthcare is the shortage of skilled workers. Hospitals, clinics, and long-term care facilities across the country are struggling to hire and retain nurses, doctors, technicians, and support staff. The COVID-19 pandemic sped up retirements, increased burnout, and drove many healthcare professionals to leave the field altogether.

According to the U.S. Bureau of Labor Statistics, the healthcare industry will need to add millions of workers over the next decade to meet rising demand. But attracting new talent is difficult. Long hours, emotional stress, and administrative burdens contribute to high turnover rates. Addressing this issue requires more than hiring—it demands better work environments, mental health support, and systemic change.

Rising Costs and Affordability

Healthcare costs in the U.S. have been rising for decades, outpacing inflation and wages. For patients, this means higher premiums, deductibles, and out-of-pocket expenses. For providers and insurers, it means pressure to cut costs without compromising quality of care.

Pharmaceutical prices, hospital services, and administrative expenses are among the key drivers of rising costs. Additionally, chronic conditions such as diabetes, heart disease, and obesity continue to increase, leading to higher long-term expenditures.

Efforts to control costs—such as value-based care, price transparency, and the use of generics—are gaining traction. But significant reform is needed to ensure that healthcare remains both high-quality and affordable for all.

Access

Access to healthcare remains a challenge, particularly for marginalized and rural populations. Millions of Americans still lack adequate insurance or live in "medical deserts" with limited access to providers. The pandemic highlighted and deepened many of these inequities.

Addressing healthcare involves expanding coverage, improving outreach, investing in community health centers, and addressing the social determinants of health—factors like housing, education, and transportation that influence well-being.

Technology Integration and Data Security

Technology is transforming healthcare—but not without challenges. The rise of Electronic Health Records (EHRs), telemedicine, wearable devices, and artificial intelligence is improving patient care and streamlining operations. However, integrating new technologies into existing systems can be complicated and costly.

Data privacy and cybersecurity are also major concerns. Healthcare organizations are prime targets for cyberattacks because of the sensitive nature of medical data. A breach can cause not only financial loss but also an erosion of patient trust.

To harness the benefits of technology while minimizing risks, healthcare providers must invest in secure, interoperable systems and ensure staff are trained in both the use and protection of digital tools.

Regulatory Complexity and Policy Uncertainty

Healthcare is one of the most heavily regulated industries. Navigating an ever-changing landscape of federal and state regulations, insurance requirements, and compliance mandates is a constant challenge for providers and administrators.

Policy uncertainty—such as debates over the Affordable Care Act, Medicare funding, or drug pricing—makes long-term planning difficult. Stability and clarity in healthcare policy are essential for innovation, investment, and the efficient delivery of services.

Conclusion

Healthcare is entering a defining era—where innovation and urgency collide. It is under pressure to provide better care to more people at a lower cost—all while adapting to rapid technological change and addressing longstanding inequities. The challenges are complex, but they also present opportunities for transformation. By investing in workforce development, embracing innovation, and enacting thoughtful policy, the healthcare industry can move forward—not just as a system for treating illness, but as a foundation for building healthier communities and a more resilient society.

Chapter Twenty

IT and Cybersecurity

The Information Technology (IT) and Cybersecurity sector is one of the fastest-growing and most critical sectors in the modern world. As businesses, governments, and individuals increasingly rely on digital infrastructure to operate, communicate, and store information, the demand for secure and reliable technology has surged. The industry is responsible not only for powering the digital economy but also for protecting it from an ever-growing array of threats.

However, the IT and cybersecurity landscape is changing rapidly—and not without challenges. From rising cyberattacks and talent shortages to regulatory complexity and technological shifts, the industry must adapt swiftly to meet the needs of an increasingly connected and vulnerable world.

Rising Cyber Threats and Sophisticated Attacks

One of the most urgent and persistent challenges facing the cybersecurity sector is the escalation of cyberthreats. Ransomware attacks, phishing scams, data breaches, and state-sponsored hacking have become alarmingly common. In 2023 alone, global ransomware attacks increased by over 70%, affecting hospitals, schools, government agencies, and major corporations.

Cybercriminals are becoming more sophisticated, using artificial intelligence (AI), deepfakes, and zero-day exploits to bypass traditional defenses. These attacks not only result in financial losses but can also compromise sensitive personal data and disrupt essential services.

With geopolitical tensions rising, nation-state cyberattacks are also on the rise, targeting critical infrastructure like energy grids, defense systems, and public health organizations. The threat landscape is constantly evolving, requiring equally agile and adaptive defense mechanisms.

Talent Shortages and Skills Gaps

Despite the high demand for IT and cybersecurity professionals, the industry faces a significant talent shortage. According to (ISC)², there is a global cybersecurity workforce gap of over 3.4 million professionals. In the United States alone, hundreds of thousands of cybersecurity positions remain unfilled.

The skills required in this field—such as ethical hacking, network defense, incident response, and risk analysis—are highly specialized, and educational institutions often struggle to keep up with industry needs. As threats grow more complex, so does the demand for experienced, well-trained professionals.

To bridge the gap, companies are turning to reskilling programs, certifications, and partnerships with educational institutions. However, attracting and retaining talent in a competitive market remains a major hurdle.

Data Privacy and Regulatory Complexity

As digital activity increases, so does the amount of personal and organizational data being collected, stored, and processed. This has led to growing concerns about data privacy and a surge in regulatory oversight.

Laws such as the European Union's General Data Protection Regulation (GDPR) and California's Consumer Privacy Act (CCPA) require businesses to handle data with strict transparency and accountability. Other countries are following suit, creating a complex patchwork of regulations that organizations must navigate.

Failure to comply can cause severe fines and reputational damage. As a result, companies must invest in compliance teams, legal expertise, and secure data management systems—adding both financial and operational burdens.

Cloud Security and Remote Work Risks

The shift to cloud computing and remote work, accelerated by the COVID-19 pandemic, has introduced new vulnerabilities. Cloud services offer scalability and flexibility but can be difficult to secure, especially if companies lack in-house expertise.

Remote work has also expanded the "attack surface" for hackers. Home networks and personal devices are often less secure than corporate environments, increasing the risk of breaches. Organizations now need to implement robust remote access policies, endpoint security, and employee training programs to mitigate these risks.

Keeping Up with Rapid Technological Change

The IT and cybersecurity fields are constantly changing. Emerging technologies like AI, quantum computing, and the Internet of Things (IoT) bring new opportunities—but also new challenges.

AI, for example, can be used both defensively and offensively. While it helps automate threat detection and response, it can also be exploited by bad actors to craft more convincing attacks. Industrial Internet of Things (IIoT) devices, many of which lack strong built-in security, create countless new entry points for hackers.

Staying ahead of these developments requires continuous investment in research, innovation, and education—something not all organizations are prepared to do.

Conclusion

The IT and cybersecurity industry is indispensable in today's digital world, but it is also under immense pressure. With cyber threats rising, regulations tightening, and technology evolving at lightning speed, the industry must be both resilient and forward-thinking. By investing in talent, embracing innovation, and fostering global collaboration, the IT and cybersecurity sector can not only meet current challenges but also shape a safer, more secure digital future for all.

Chapter Twenty-One

Manufacturing

The manufacturing industry has long been a driving force of economic growth, innovation, and job creation. From cars and electronics to machinery and consumer goods, manufacturing powers much of the global economy and provides the infrastructure for other sectors to thrive. In the United States alone, the manufacturing sector contributes over $2.3 trillion to the economy annually and employs nearly 13 million people.

However, presently, the manufacturing industry finds itself at a critical juncture. Faced with a rapidly changing global environment, manufacturers are grappling with a host of complex challenges that impact production, profitability, and long-term competitiveness.

Labor Shortages and Skills Gaps

One of the most pressing issues facing the manufacturing industry today is a shortage of skilled labor. As experienced workers retire, there simply aren't enough younger workers entering the field to replace them. According to the National Association of Manufacturers (NAM), over 2.1 million manufacturing jobs in the U.S. could go unfilled by 2030 if current trends continue.

The challenge isn't just a lack of workers—it's a lack of workers with the right skills. Modern manufacturing increasingly requires expertise in robotics, data analysis, and automation. However, public perception still views manufacturing as dirty, low-tech, and physically demanding, discouraging many young people from pursuing careers in the field.

To address the gap, companies are investing in workforce development initiatives, partnering with community colleges, and promoting apprenticeships to upskill new talent. Still, cultural attitudes and outdated stereotypes remain significant hurdles.

Supply Chain Disruptions

The COVID-19 pandemic and subsequent global events exposed significant vulnerabilities in the manufacturing supply chain. From raw material shortages to shipping delays and port congestion, manufacturers have faced persistent disruptions that challenge just-in-time production models.

Geopolitical tensions, such as trade disputes and military conflicts, have added further strain, especially for companies reliant on international suppliers. Manufacturers are now reevaluating their supply chains, exploring reshoring (bringing production back to domestic locations) and nearshoring (relocating to nearby countries) to increase resilience and reduce dependence on global logistics.

However, reconfiguring supply chains is a complex and costly process, especially for small and mid-sized manufacturers with limited resources.

Technological Transformation and Industry 4.0

The manufacturing sector is undergoing a digital revolution, often referred to as Industry 4.0. This includes the integration of technologies such as artificial intelligence (AI), the Industrial Internet of Things (IIoT), additive manufacturing (3D printing), and smart sensors to enhance production efficiency and data-driven decision-making.

While these innovations offer huge potential benefits, they also bring challenges. Many manufacturers—especially smaller firms—struggle with the cost of upgrading legacy systems or lack the technical expertise to implement new technologies effectively. Cybersecurity concerns also rise as more systems become interconnected.

To remain competitive, manufacturers must embrace digital transformation while managing the risks and complexities that come with it.

Environmental Pressures and Sustainability Goals

As the world focuses more on environmental sustainability, manufacturers are under increasing pressure to reduce emissions, improve energy efficiency, and minimize waste. Consumers, investors, and governments are demanding more transparent and eco-friendly practices throughout the supply chain.

Regulatory requirements are also tightening. From carbon taxes to emissions reporting mandates, manufacturers must now comply with a growing list of environmental standards. While these efforts support long-term sustainability, they often require significant upfront investments in new technologies and processes.

Global Competition and Economic Uncertainty

Manufacturers today operate in a fiercely competitive global marketplace. Emerging economies continue to offer lower labor costs, putting pressure on domestic producers to innovate and differentiate through quality, customization, and speed.

Economic uncertainty—driven by inflation, fluctuating interest rates, and shifting trade policies—makes planning and investment more difficult. In this unpredictable environment, adaptability and strategic agility are essential.

Conclusion

The manufacturing industry is undergoing a transformative shift. As it faces mounting challenges—from labor shortages and supply chain disruptions to technological and environmental shifts—it must also seize the opportunities that change brings. By investing in people, embracing innovation, and building more resilient and sustainable operations, manufacturers can not only overcome today's challenges but also shape the future of the global industry. The path forward will require collaboration, creativity, and a renewed focus on the value manufacturing brings to the economy, society, and everyday life.

Chapter Twenty-Two

Mining

The mining industry has long been a cornerstone of global economic development, providing the raw materials that fuel infrastructure, energy, technology, and manufacturing. From copper and lithium used in electric vehicles to iron and coal essential for construction and power generation, mining underpins virtually every major industry. However, the mining sector is facing a complex array of challenges that are reshaping its operations, economics, and environmental responsibilities.

As the world transitions to a greener and more digital future, the demand for minerals is increasing. Yet, the path to meeting that demand is becoming more difficult and costly. Issues such as environmental regulations, labor shortages, community opposition, and geopolitical risk are pressuring companies to rethink how they extract, process, and deliver the materials the world depends on.

Environmental Pressures and Sustainability Demands

One of the most pressing challenges for the mining industry is the growing demand for environmental sustainability. Mining has traditionally been associated with deforestation, water pollution, and greenhouse gas emissions—leading to increased scrutiny from governments, investors, and the public.

Regulations are tightening around emissions, land use, and waste management. Companies are now required to conduct more extensive environmental impact assessments and invest in mitigation strategies, such as land reclamation and water recycling.

At the same time, there's a paradox at play: the transition to renewable energy and electric vehicles is increasing demand for minerals like lithium, cobalt, and nickel—materials that must be mined. The industry must now mine more sustainably while satisfying a global push for clean energy.

Social License to Operate and Community Relations

Securing a "social license to operate" is becoming more difficult for mining companies. Local communities, Indigenous groups, and environmental organizations are increasingly vocal about the potential effects of mining projects on land, water, and livelihoods.

Sometimes, opposition has led to legal delays or outright cancellations of projects. Gaining community trust and approval requires companies to engage in transparent dialogue, ensure fair compensation, and commit to local development initiatives.

Respecting Indigenous rights and ensuring meaningful consultation is not only an ethical responsibility but also a legal requirement in many jurisdictions. Failing to do so can jeopardize operations and damage corporate reputations.

Resource Depletion and Access Challenges

Many of the world's richest mineral deposits have already been tapped, meaning new exploration efforts must reach deeper, more remote, or geologically complex areas. This increases operational costs and technical challenges.

In addition, geopolitical instability and resource nationalism—where countries impose stricter control over their natural resources—are making access more difficult. Nations such as Indonesia, Chile, and the Democratic Republic of Congo have introduced new taxes, export restrictions, or nationalization measures aimed at retaining greater economic benefits from their mineral wealth.

These trends add layers of complexity to global supply chains and investment strategies for mining companies.

Labor Shortages and Skills Gaps

Like many other sectors, the mining industry is facing labor shortages and a growing skills gap. As older workers retire, companies are struggling to attract younger talent to what is often perceived as a physically demanding and environmentally harmful industry.

The rise of automation and digital mining technologies requires a new type of workforce—one skilled in data analytics, robotics, and remote operations. Upskilling the current workforce and making the industry more attractive to younger, tech-savvy employees is essential for future success.

Technological Transformation and Digitalization

While digital technology offers solutions to many mining challenges—improving safety, increasing efficiency, and reducing environmental impact—implementing these technologies is not without obstacles.

High costs, lack of digital infrastructure in remote areas, and resistance to change within organizations can hinder progress. Nonetheless, innovations such as autonomous vehicles, drone surveying, and real-time data analytics are reshaping the industry and helping it operate more sustainably and productively.

Conclusion

The mining industry is facing significant changes. As global demand for critical minerals grows, so too does the pressure to mine responsibly, ethically, and efficiently. The sector must balance economic opportunity with environmental stewardship, community engagement, and technological innovation. Meeting these challenges will require collaboration across governments, industry, and civil society. Those mining companies that can adapt to the new landscape—by embracing sustainability, leveraging technology, and fostering strong community relations—will be best positioned to thrive in the future of resource extraction.

Chapter Twenty-Three

Skilled Trades

T he skilled trades industry—comprising electricians, plumbers, welders, HVAC technicians, machinists, carpenters, and more—is the backbone of modern infrastructure and daily life. From maintaining power grids and plumbing systems to constructing homes and repairing vehicles, skilled trades professionals keep society running smoothly. Despite its essential role, the industry is facing a host of challenges that threaten its future, workforce sustainability, and ability to meet growing demand.

As the economy evolves and the population increases, the demand for trade skills increases. The skilled trades sector must confront critical issues such as labor shortages, generational perceptions, education gaps, and technological transformation.

Severe Labor Shortages

One of the most pressing challenges for the skilled trades industry is a widespread labor shortage. According to the U.S. Bureau of Labor Statistics, hundreds of thousands of skilled trade jobs remain unfilled, and this number is expected to grow in the coming decade. The National Association of Home Builders, for instance, reports that over 80% of its members face a shortage of qualified labor.

Several factors contribute to this shortfall. Many experienced tradespeople from the baby boomer generation are retiring, and not enough younger workers are entering the field to replace them. This widening gap is causing delays, increasing costs for contractors, and hindering economic growth in sectors reliant on skilled labor.

Negative Perceptions and Cultural Bias

A major obstacle in attracting new talent to the skilled trades is the persistent societal bias that favors four-year college degrees over vocational education. For decades, students have been encouraged to pursue academic paths, often overlooking or being discouraged from entering the trades.

As a result, many young people and their families are unaware of the benefits of a career in the trades—including competitive pay, job stability, career advancement opportunities, and the ability to work without accumulating significant student debt.

Changing these perceptions requires a cultural shift in how society values and promotes vocational education. Schools, parents, and policymakers must work together to elevate the status of trade-related occupations and communicate their importance and potential.

Education and Training Barriers

While there is strong demand for skilled workers, access to quality training programs remains uneven. Many high schools have reduced or eliminated shop classes and vocational training over the years, limiting early exposure to trade careers. In some regions, community colleges and technical schools lack sufficient funding or industry partnerships to provide up-to-date, hands-on instruction.

Apprenticeship programs—which combine classroom learning with paid, on-the-job training—are a proven pathway into the trades, but they are underutilized and often misunderstood. Expanding and modernizing these programs can help bridge the gap between education and employment.

Technological Advancements and Adaptation

Like other industries, the skilled trades are being transformed by technology. Innovations in tools, equipment, and techniques are improving efficiency and safety, but they also require workers to continuously update their skills.

For example, electricians now install smart home systems, HVAC technicians work with energy-efficient and AI-controlled systems, and welders may use robotic machinery. Tradespeople must not only be experts in their craft but also comfortable with digital tools, diagnostics, and automation.

This evolution presents both a challenge and an opportunity. Workers and employers must invest in ongoing education and embrace a mindset of lifelong learning to stay competitive in a rapidly changing industry.

Conclusion

The skilled trades industry is essential to building, maintaining, and powering the world we live in—but its long-term future is fragile. Addressing labor shortages, changing cultural perceptions, improving access to training, and embracing new technology are all critical to ensuring the industry's resilience and growth. By investing in people, promoting vocational pathways, and fostering a culture of respect for skilled work, the trades can attract a new generation of workers ready to build the future—literally and figuratively.

Chapter Twenty-Four

Supply Chain and Logistics

T he supply chain and logistics sector is the invisible engine of the global economy, responsible for moving goods from manufacturers to consumers with precision and speed. From sourcing raw materials and managing inventory to transportation, warehousing, and last-mile delivery, this complex network underpins everything from grocery store shelves to international trade.

However, in recent years, the sector has faced an unprecedented wave of disruption. The COVID-19 pandemic exposed deep vulnerabilities in global supply chains, and recovery has been difficult. Now, the industry must adapt to new economic, environmental, and geopolitical realities that are reshaping how goods move around the world.

Global Disruptions and Fragile Networks

The pandemic was a wake-up call for the supply chain and logistics industry. Factory shutdowns, port congestion, container shortages, and labor disruptions created massive backlogs and delivery delays across the globe. Even as the immediate crisis has subsided, the ripple effects remain.

Further complicating recovery are events like the war in Ukraine, which has disrupted critical trade routes and the supply of key materials like grain and energy, and tensions in the Red Sea and South China Sea, which affect maritime shipping lanes. The once-lean, just-in-time supply chain model is being reevaluated as companies look for ways to build more resilient and flexible networks.

Labor Shortages Across the Chain

From truck drivers and warehouse workers to freight handlers and logistics planners, labor shortages are a significant challenge throughout the supply chain. The trucking industry in the U.S. faces a shortage of over 80,000 drivers, according to the American Trucking Associations.

These shortages have been driven by several factors: an aging workforce, difficult working conditions, rising demand for e-commerce, and the lack of new talent entering the field. Warehousing and distribution centers also struggle to keep staff because of long hours, physically demanding tasks, and competition from other industries.

To address these shortages, companies are investing in better pay, automation, and workforce development programs—but solutions will take time.

Technology Gaps and Digital Transformation

Technology plays a critical role in modern supply chain management, offering tools for tracking shipments, forecasting demand, and optimizing routes. However, many companies—particularly small and mid-sized ones—still rely on outdated systems or manual processes.

The push toward digital transformation includes the adoption of technologies like cloud-based logistics platforms, artificial intelligence (AI), blockchain for tracking provenance, and the Industrial Internet of Things (IIoT) for real-time asset monitoring. These tools can improve visibility, efficiency, and decision-making—but implementing them is costly and requires skilled personnel.

Cybersecurity is also a growing concern, as supply chains become more digitally interconnected and vulnerable to cyberattacks that can disrupt operations and compromise sensitive data.

Sustainability and Environmental Pressures

Sustainability has become a key priority for the supply chain and logistics sector. As global awareness of climate change grows, companies are under increasing pressure from consumers, investors, and regulators to reduce emissions, minimize waste, and adopt greener practices.

Transportation is a major source of greenhouse gas emissions, and many firms are exploring alternative fuels, electric vehicles, and more efficient delivery methods to shrink their carbon footprint. Warehousing and packaging are also being reexamined for energy efficiency and recyclability.

However, achieving sustainability goals often comes with high upfront costs and logistical complexity—especially when trying to balance environmental performance with speed and cost-effectiveness.

Geopolitical Risks and Trade Policy Uncertainty

Global trade is deeply influenced by geopolitics, and recent years have seen rising protectionism, tariffs, and export controls that impact supply chains. The U.S.-China trade tensions, Brexit, and sanctions on countries like Russia have forced companies to rethink sourcing strategies and diversify their supplier bases.

The trend toward "nearshoring" and "reshoring"—moving production closer to home—is growing as companies seek to reduce risk and improve control. While this adds resilience, it also increases costs and requires major logistical adjustments.

Conclusion

The supply chain and logistics sector is amid a profound transformation. What was once a behind-the-scenes operation is now front and center of discussions about economic resilience, sustainability, and national security. To overcome current and future challenges, the industry must embrace innovation, invest in its workforce, and redesign systems for greater adaptability and transparency. Those who succeed will not only weather disruptions but build stronger, smarter, and more sustainable supply chains for the future.

Chapter Twenty-Five

Technology

The technology sector has long been a driving force behind global economic growth, innovation, and societal transformation. From cloud computing and artificial intelligence (AI) to smartphones and social media, technological advancements have reshaped the way we live, work, and connect. Yet, despite its reputation for rapid growth and disruption, the technology industry is facing a range of significant challenges that are testing its resilience and adaptability.

While innovation remains the cornerstone of the sector, it must now navigate shifting global dynamics, regulatory pressures, workforce disruptions, and ethical concerns that could redefine its trajectory in the years ahead.

Economic Uncertainty and Market Volatility

After a decade of vigorous growth, the technology industry is experiencing increased market volatility. Rising interest rates, inflation, and geopolitical instability have led to tighter capital markets, making it harder for startups to raise funding and for large tech companies to sustain aggressive expansion strategies.

Many firms have responded with cost-cutting measures, including hiring freezes, layoffs, and scaled-back investment in research and development. This economic climate is forcing the sector to focus more on operational efficiency and profitability than on unchecked growth.

The challenge now is balancing innovation with financial discipline—an unfamiliar terrain for an industry built on bold bets and long-term disruption.

Regulatory Scrutiny and Antitrust Pressure

Governments around the world are increasingly scrutinizing the power and influence of large tech companies. From the U.S. and Europe to Asia, regulators are introducing new laws aimed at addressing antitrust concerns, data privacy, misinformation, and content moderation.

Legislation like the European Union's Digital Markets Act and the Digital Services Act, as well as efforts in the U.S. to rein in monopolistic practices, are forcing tech giants to rethink business models, particularly those built on data-driven advertising and platform dominance.

At the same time, smaller tech companies must navigate a patchwork of global regulations that can be burdensome and costly. Ensuring compliance while maintaining innovation is a delicate balancing act.

Cybersecurity Threats and Data Privacy Concerns

As the world becomes more digitally connected, cybersecurity risks are escalating. High-profile data breaches, ransomware attacks, and state-sponsored cyber espionage have become increasingly common, threatening both companies and consumers.

The technology sector must remain at the forefront of cybersecurity innovation while simultaneously protecting user data and maintaining trust. Consumers and businesses alike are demanding more transparency and stronger protections for data collection, storage, and usage.

In addition, new technologies like AI and the Industrial Internet of Things (IIoT) are creating more entry points for cyberattacks, increasing the need for robust security protocols and industry-wide collaboration.

Talent Shortages and Workforce Challenges

Despite high interest in tech careers, the sector is facing a growing talent gap—particularly in areas such as cybersecurity, software development, data science, and AI. Competition for top talent is fierce, and many companies struggle to attract and retain skilled workers.

The rapid pace of technological change means that the demand for new skills often outpaces the supply. Upskilling and reskilling initiatives are essential, but many organizations lack the infrastructure or long-term planning to implement them effectively.

Additionally, the shift to remote and hybrid work models has introduced both flexibility and complexity. Building cohesive teams, maintaining collaboration, and managing productivity in decentralized environments require new leadership and communication strategies.

Ethical Dilemmas and Social Responsibility

As technology becomes more embedded in daily life, ethical concerns have taken center stage. Issues such as algorithmic bias, misinformation on social media platforms, the environmental impact of data centers, and the responsible use of AI are sparking public debate and regulatory action.

Consumers and employees alike expect technology companies to act responsibly, uphold human rights, and consider the broader societal implications of their products. The industry must develop frameworks for ethical innovation and ensure accountability at all levels.

Conclusion

The technology sector is entering a new era—one that demands more than innovation alone. From navigating economic headwinds and regulatory scrutiny to addressing cybersecurity, workforce gaps, and ethical concerns, the challenges are as complex as they are consequential. Yet within these challenges lie opportunities: to build more responsible, inclusive, and resilient technologies that shape a better future. For companies that can adapt, lead with purpose, and prioritize long-term value over short-term gains, the next wave of innovation may be the most impactful yet.

Section 4: 5 Areas of Impact In Manufacturing

Chapter Twenty-Six

Workplace Safety

Workplace safety is a top priority in the manufacturing industry, where employees regularly operate heavy machinery, handle hazardous materials, and perform physically demanding tasks. While safety protocols, regulations, and equipment all play a crucial role, one of the most effective and sustainable ways to ensure a safe work environment is through workforce development. Investing in the training, education, and ongoing development of employees directly enhances their ability to recognize hazards, follow safety procedures, and respond effectively to emergencies—ultimately reducing the risk of accidents and injuries on the job.

Training That Prevents Accidents

One of the leading causes of workplace injuries in manufacturing is human error, often stemming from inadequate training. When workers don't fully understand how to operate machinery, handle materials, or follow safety protocols, the likelihood of accidents increases significantly.

Through comprehensive workforce development, employees receive hands-on training in the correct operation of equipment, proper use of Personal Protective Equipment (PPE), lockout/tagout (LOTO) procedures, and other essential safety practices. This training ensures that safety becomes second nature to every worker, reducing the chances of errors that could lead to injury or property damage.

Promoting a Safety-First Culture

Workforce development also plays a critical role in building a strong safety culture. When employees are consistently trained and retrained on safety standards, they internalize those practices as part of their daily routines. They become more aware of their surroundings, more accountable for their actions, and more likely to look out for one another.

A safety-first culture encourages open communication about hazards, near misses, and safety concerns. Through workforce development programs such as team-building exercises, toolbox talks, and peer-led training sessions, workers become active participants in maintaining a safe environment rather than passive recipients of top-down rules.

Empowering Supervisors and Leaders

Supervisors and team leaders have a significant impact on workplace safety. When these leaders are well-trained in safety protocols and communication skills, they can more effectively identify risks, enforce safety standards, and mentor their teams. Workforce development programs that focus on leadership skills ensure supervisors are equipped to manage safety proactively, rather than reacting to incidents after they occur.

By creating a pipeline of safety-conscious leaders, manufacturers can ensure that every level of the organization is aligned in its commitment to workplace safety.

Adapting to New Technologies and Standards

The manufacturing industry is constantly evolving, with new technologies, machinery, and regulatory standards being introduced regularly. Without ongoing workforce development, employees may struggle to adapt to these changes safely. For example, new automated systems or robotics require different safety considerations than traditional machinery.

Training programs help workers stay up-to-date with the latest safety standards, learn how to interact with new equipment, and understand how evolving processes may affect workplace hazards. This adaptability is essential for maintaining safety as the industry advances.

Reducing Costs and Improving Morale

In addition to protecting workers, improving safety through workforce development has direct financial benefits. Fewer accidents mean lower medical costs, reduced workers' compensation claims, and less downtime. It also improves morale and retention—employees are more likely to stay with companies that prioritize their well-being and invest in their development.

When workers feel safe and supported, they are more focused, productive, and engaged, leading to a healthier and more successful workplace overall.

Conclusion

Workforce development is a powerful tool for improving organizational safety. By equipping employees with the knowledge, skills, and mindset to work safely, companies can prevent accidents, foster a culture of safety, and adapt to an ever-changing industrial landscape. In the end, developing people is not just good for business—it's essential for keeping everyone safe.

Chapter Twenty-Seven

Morale and Culture

I n the fast-paced and often physically demanding environment of
the manufacturing industry, company culture and employee morale
play vital roles in productivity, retention, and overall workplace success.
While many organizations focus on safety and efficiency, a growing
number of manufacturers are recognizing the powerful impact of workforce development on morale and company culture. When employees
feel valued, supported, and empowered to grow, it transforms the workplace from a job site into a community—boosting motivation, loyalty,
and long-term success.

Building a Culture of Growth and Opportunity

One of the most powerful ways workforce development improves morale
is by creating a culture of growth. When employees see their employer
will invest in their skills and future, they feel valued and supported. This
builds trust and loyalty, which are essential ingredients for a positive
company culture.

In manufacturing, where frontline roles are sometimes perceived as static
or limited in growth opportunities, training and upskilling programs
show that advancement is possible. Whether it's learning how to operate
new machinery, moving into a supervisory role, or taking part in lean
manufacturing projects, these opportunities show workers that they have
a future beyond their current position.

Enhancing Communication and Teamwork

A strong culture is rooted in strong relationships, and workforce development supports this by enhancing communication and teamwork.

Training programs often bring employees together across departments or shifts, encouraging collaboration and shared problem-solving. Leadership development programs can also teach supervisors how to engage their teams more effectively, manage conflict, and give constructive feedback.

When communication improves, so does morale. Employees feel heard, respected, and more connected to their coworkers. A culture of openness and collaboration replaces one of hierarchy and isolation, making the workplace more enjoyable and productive.

Empowering Employees Through Skill-Building

Manufacturing roles require a wide range of skills, and when employees are equipped to do their jobs well, it boosts their confidence and job satisfaction. Workforce development helps workers master the tools, techniques, and technologies they need to succeed. With every new skill gained, employees gain a sense of accomplishment and pride in their work.

This empowerment translates into higher morale. Employees who feel competent and capable are more likely to be engaged, proactive, and invested in the company's success. They're also more likely to take initiative, contribute ideas, and help improve processes—further reinforcing a culture of innovation and continuous improvement.

Reducing Turnover and Building Loyalty

Low morale often leads to high turnover, which is costly and disruptive. Conversely, workforce development helps reduce turnover by demonstrating that the company values its people. When employees are given a clear path to grow, along with the tools to get there, they're more likely to stay and build a long-term career.

This stability supports a strong, consistent culture. Veteran employees serve as mentors, pass on institutional knowledge, and help shape the workplace environment for the better.

Conclusion

In the manufacturing industry, workforce development is more than a productivity strategy—it's a culture-building investment. By supporting employee growth, improving communication, and creating pathways for advancement, workforce development boosts morale and fosters a workplace culture rooted in respect, opportunity, and shared success. In a competitive labor market, manufacturers that prioritize people development don't just attract talent—they build thriving, engaged teams that drive the company forward.

Chapter Twenty-Eight

Quality and Efficiency

I n the manufacturing industry, success is measured by how well companies can produce high-quality goods quickly, consistently, and cost-effectively. With global competition intensifying and customer expectations rising, manufacturers are under increasing pressure to deliver flawless products with minimal waste and downtime. One of the most powerful and sustainable ways to meet these demands is through workforce development. By investing in employee training, education, and upskilling, manufacturers can significantly improve both product quality and operational efficiency.

Improving Product Quality

A skilled workforce is essential to producing high-quality products. When employees are properly trained, they understand how to operate equipment accurately, follow standard operating procedures, and identify defects or issues early in the production process. This reduces errors, rework, and scrap—ultimately lowering costs and improving customer satisfaction.

For example, a machine operator who understands the precise tolerances required for a part can make real-time adjustments to avoid production errors. A quality control technician with the right training can spot inconsistencies before products move down the line, preventing defective items from reaching customers.

In industries such as automotive, aerospace, and medical device manufacturing—where precision is critical and regulations are strict—training and certification in quality standards such as ISO 9001 or Six Sigma methodologies can make a significant difference in maintaining high-quality outputs.

Boosting Operational Efficiency

Efficiency in manufacturing means producing more with less: less time, less waste, and fewer resources. Workforce development helps companies achieve this by equipping employees with the skills to work smarter, not just harder.

Cross-training employees to handle multiple roles reduces downtime caused by absences or turnover. Lean manufacturing training helps teams identify and eliminate waste in production processes. Digital literacy and automation training prepares workers to work alongside advanced technologies like robotics and smart sensors, which improve production speed and data accuracy.

Moreover, when employees are empowered to understand the "why" behind their tasks—not just the "how"—they become more engaged and proactive. They are more likely to suggest process improvements, take ownership of their performance, and work collaboratively to resolve bottlenecks.

Enhancing Problem-Solving and Continuous Improvement

Manufacturing environments are dynamic, and problems can arise quickly—whether it's a machine malfunction, a supply chain disruption, or a production delay. A well-trained workforce is better equipped to diagnose problems, find solutions, and implement corrective actions without unnecessary delays.

Workforce development programs that include critical thinking and root cause analysis prepare employees to solve problems at the source rather than applying temporary fixes. This mindset of continuous improvement contributes to greater long-term efficiency and product consistency.

Supporting Innovation and Adaptability

Modern manufacturing is changing rapidly with the adoption of Industry 4.0 technologies such as the Industrial Internet of Things (IIoT), artificial intelligence, and cloud-based production systems. These advancements promise greater efficiency and quality, but only if the workforce is prepared to use them effectively.

Workforce development bridges the gap between new technology and real-world applications. It ensures that workers are not only comfortable with new tools but can also adapt to changing processes, systems, and market demands.

Conclusion

Quality and efficiency combine as the foundation of manufacturing success—and both are driven by people. Workforce development equips employees with the knowledge, skills, and confidence to do their jobs better, faster, and with fewer errors. It fosters a culture of excellence, innovation, and accountability that permeates every aspect of production. In an industry where precision and speed matter, investing in your workforce is one of the smartest and most impactful decisions a manufacturer can make.

Chapter Twenty-Nine

Uptime and Productivity

I n the manufacturing industry, uptime and productivity are key performance indicators that directly impact profitability and customer satisfaction. Equipment that runs smoothly and employees who perform efficiently ensure that production targets are met, waste is minimized, and costs stay under control. But achieving consistent uptime and high productivity doesn't happen by accident—it starts with people. Workforce development plays a critical role in ensuring that manufacturers have the skilled, knowledgeable, and engaged employees needed to maintain operations and drive performance forward.

Reducing Equipment Downtime

Unplanned downtime is one of the costliest issues manufacturers face. Whether it's because of equipment failure, operator error, or a lack of proper maintenance, downtime can halt production, delay orders, and increase operational costs.

Workforce development helps reduce downtime by training employees to operate equipment correctly and perform preventative maintenance tasks. A skilled machine operator knows how to recognize early signs of mechanical issues and take corrective action before a breakdown occurs. Similarly, maintenance technicians with up-to-date training can service equipment efficiently and spot problems during routine inspections.

Investing in training also ensures that more employees are cross-trained to handle various machines and processes. This flexibility helps fill gaps when key workers are unavailable, keeping production running smoothly and without delays.

Boosting Productivity Through Skill and Confidence

Productivity in manufacturing is not just about working faster—it's about working smarter. Workforce development helps employees gain the knowledge and confidence to do their jobs with precision and efficiency. Well-trained employees make fewer mistakes, require less supervision, and are better at managing their time and resources.

For instance, an employee trained in lean manufacturing principles can identify and eliminate waste in workflows, while a team member with strong troubleshooting skills can resolve issues quickly without waiting for managerial intervention.

Additionally, employees who feel competent in their roles are more likely to stay engaged and motivated, which further boosts productivity. They take pride in their work, strive for continuous improvement, and are more open to adopting new methods or technologies.

Enhancing Workflow and Team Collaboration

Effective manufacturing relies heavily on coordination and communication among different teams. Workforce development programs that include soft skills training—such as communication, teamwork, and problem-solving—foster a more collaborative environment. When employees communicate effectively, production schedules are better understood, roles are clearly defined, and issues are resolved faster.

Supervisory and leadership training also contributes to improved productivity by equipping managers with the tools to motivate teams, manage performance, and streamline operations.

Supporting Digital Transformation

As manufacturing embraces automation, robotics, and data-driven technologies, the demand for tech-savvy workers has grown significantly. Workforce development is the bridge that helps employees keep pace with digital transformation. Through targeted training, workers can learn to use new software, operate smart machines, and interpret real-time production data to make faster, better decisions.

A digitally fluent workforce is not only more productive—it also ensures that manufacturers can fully leverage the efficiency gains promised by Industry 4.0 technologies.

Creating a Culture of Continuous Improvement

One of the long-term benefits of workforce development is the creation of a culture where learning, growth, and innovation are encouraged. In such environments, employees are empowered to suggest improvements, take initiative, and contribute to higher levels of performance across the organization.

This culture helps manufacturers stay competitive, agile, and prepared for future challenges, including changes in demand, supply chain disruptions, or shifts in customer expectations.

Conclusion

In the manufacturing industry, uptime and productivity are the lifeblood of success. Workforce development is a strategic investment that equips employees with the skills, confidence, and mindset needed to minimize downtime and maximize output. By training and empowering workers, manufacturers not only strengthen their operations—they build a resilient, efficient, and high-performing organization ready for the demands of the modern market.

Chapter Thirty

Global Competitiveness

I n a world where innovation, speed, and quality are the benchmarks of industrial success, the global competitiveness of a nation's manufacturing sector is more important than ever. As countries race to modernize their factories, adopt new technologies, and meet growing customer demands, one critical factor stands out: a skilled, adaptable, and future-ready workforce. Workforce development has emerged as a key driver of global competitiveness in the manufacturing industry, helping companies enhance productivity, innovate faster, and maintain a sound position in international markets.

Enhancing Productivity and Efficiency

Skilled workers are more productive and efficient, allowing manufacturers to meet tight deadlines, reduce waste, and improve overall output. When employees are trained to operate machinery properly, follow best practices, and implement lean manufacturing techniques, production processes become faster and more reliable.

This level of efficiency is vital in a global market where customers expect faster turnaround times and just-in-time delivery. Countries and companies with a well-developed manufacturing workforce are better positioned to meet these demands, helping them outperform international competitors in both cost and speed.

Driving Innovation and Technological Advancement

Innovation is at the heart of global competitiveness, and a well-trained workforce is essential for driving it. As Industry 4.0 technologies like automation, artificial intelligence, robotics, and the Industrial Internet of Things (IIoT) reshape the manufacturing landscape, workers must possess the digital skills and technical knowledge to operate, manage, and improve these systems.

Workforce development programs that focus on emerging technologies enable manufacturers to adopt and integrate cutting-edge solutions faster than their competitors. When employees are comfortable with new tools and technologies, manufacturers can stay ahead of the innovation curve and bring new products to market more quickly—an undeniable advantage in the global economy.

Improving Quality and Customer Satisfaction

In global markets, reputation matters. Poor product quality can cause lost contracts, damaged relationships, and a reduced market share. Skilled workers are more likely to produce high-quality products consistently, as they understand the importance of precision, standards, and attention to detail.

Workforce development programs that include quality control training, certifications (such as ISO 9001 or Six Sigma), and continuous improvement methodologies ensure employees uphold the highest manufacturing standards. This leads to greater customer satisfaction, repeat business, and a stronger brand reputation internationally.

Attracting Investment and Strengthening Supply Chains

Countries and regions that invest in workforce development are more attractive to manufacturers and investors. A skilled labor pool reduces the risks and costs associated with establishing new operations, encouraging both domestic expansion and foreign direct investment.

Additionally, workforce development helps stabilize and strengthen supply chains by ensuring that every link—from suppliers to assembly lines—has the talent needed to meet demand. This resilience and reliability are essential in a competitive global environment where disruptions can quickly derail production.

Conclusion

In today's global manufacturing landscape, workforce development is not a luxury—it is a necessity. By investing in the skills and growth of their employees, manufacturers gain the agility, innovation, quality, and efficiency required to compete on the world stage. As technologies continue to change and competition intensifies, those who prioritize workforce development will be the ones who lead—not just locally, but globally. For any manufacturing company or country looking to secure its place in the global market, the smartest move is clear: invest in your people.

Section 5: 5 Areas of Impact In Defense

Chapter Thirty-One

National Security

I n an increasingly interconnected and technology-driven world, national security depends on far more than military strength alone. Cybersecurity, supply chain integrity, critical infrastructure, and technological innovation are all vital components of a secure nation—and each of these areas requires a highly skilled, capable workforce. Bridging the growing skills gap in the U.S. isn't just an economic priority; It's a national security imperative.

The skills gap refers to the mismatch between the skills employers need and the qualifications that job seekers possess. This gap is especially pronounced in critical sectors like cybersecurity, advanced manufacturing, defense technology, and engineering. When these essential roles go unfilled or are staffed by underqualified personnel, it leaves the U.S. vulnerable to internal and external threats.

Cybersecurity: The Frontline of Modern Defense

One of the most pressing areas affected by the skills gap is cybersecurity. As cyberattacks from foreign adversaries grow more sophisticated, the demand for cybersecurity professionals continues to outpace supply. The U.S. currently has hundreds of thousands of unfilled cybersecurity jobs—a shortfall that directly affects national defense.

Bridging this gap through workforce development, education, and public-private partnerships is essential to building a strong digital defense. Training programs focused on ethical hacking, data protection, risk analysis, and cyber forensics help prepare a new generation of cyber warriors who can secure government systems, critical infrastructure, and private industry from persistent threats.

Strengthening Defense and Intelligence Capabilities

In the defense and intelligence sectors, national security increasingly depends on technological innovation. Emerging technologies such as artificial intelligence, quantum computing, drone technology, and autonomous systems are transforming how wars are fought and information is gathered.

However, to lead in these fields, the U.S. needs scientists, engineers, and technical experts who are proficient in advanced technologies. Bridging the STEM skills gap ensures that the Department of Defense and intelligence agencies can develop and deploy cutting-edge systems while staying ahead of global competitors like China and Russia.

Moreover, having a pipeline of homegrown talent reduces the need to rely on foreign expertise, which can raise security concerns about access to sensitive data and technologies.

Securing Critical Infrastructure

National security also hinges on the resilience of critical infrastructure—including energy grids, transportation systems, water supplies, and healthcare networks. These sectors are increasingly connected and digitized, requiring skilled workers to operate, maintain, and secure them.

A shortage of qualified technicians, IT specialists, and engineers in these industries can lead to vulnerabilities that malicious actors could exploit. Bridging the skills gap ensures that these vital systems are protected from sabotage, cyberattacks, and other disruptions.

Building a Resilient, Ready Workforce

Beyond defense, a secure nation needs a resilient workforce capable of responding to emergencies, pandemics, and natural disasters. Workforce development that includes emergency response training, logistics coordination, and health services preparedness equips individuals with the skills needed to keep communities safe and operational during crises.

Programs like apprenticeships, vocational training, and military-to-civilian transition initiatives help expand the talent pool and ensure that skilled professionals are ready when the country needs them most.

Conclusion

Bridging the skills gap isn't just about jobs—it's about securing the future of the United States. National security today depends on a robust, adaptable, and skilled workforce across multiple sectors. By investing in education, training, and workforce development, the U.S. strengthens its ability to defend against modern threats, maintain global leadership in technology and defense, and protect the systems that keep the country running. Closing the skills gap is a national security strategy in its own right—and one we cannot afford to ignore.

Chapter Thirty-Two

Competitive Innovation

The U.S. Department of Defense (DoD) has long been a global leader in technological advancement, responsible for pioneering innovations that not only strengthen national security but also influence industries beyond the military. From GPS technology to stealth aircraft and advanced cyber capabilities, the DoD's ability to innovate is central to its strategic advantage. However, that advantage is now being challenged by a growing threat from within: the widening skills gap.

Bridging the skills gap in the defense workforce is essential to maintaining and accelerating innovation. As emerging technologies reshape modern warfare—artificial intelligence (AI), cybersecurity, hypersonics, space operations, and autonomous systems—the DoD must have access to a highly skilled, adaptable workforce. Without it, the department risks falling behind near-peer adversaries in both technological capability and strategic readiness.

Fueling Innovation with Skilled Talent

Competitive innovation begins with skilled people. Scientists, engineers, and technologists form the backbone of research and development efforts in the DoD. These professionals drive progress in weapons systems, secure communications, AI applications, robotics, and more. When the workforce is equipped with cutting-edge knowledge and capabilities, innovation accelerates.

Bridging the skills gap ensures the DoD can continue to lead in developing technologies that provide strategic advantages on the battlefield. It enables faster prototyping, smoother integration of new systems, and more effective collaboration with private-sector partners and research institutions.

Furthermore, having in-house expertise allows the DoD to maintain control over sensitive technologies, reducing the risks associated with outsourcing innovation to foreign or unvetted third-party vendors.

Competing with Global Adversaries

Global competitors like China and Russia are making aggressive investments in military technology and STEM education. These nations are rapidly modernizing their defense capabilities, aiming to close the technological gap with the United States—or surpass it.

Bridging the skills gap is a necessary response to this challenge. It ensures that the U.S. remains on the cutting edge of defense innovation and maintains superiority in areas like AI-driven surveillance, electronic warfare, missile defense, and space operations.

A highly skilled workforce also gives the U.S. the flexibility to explore and develop unconventional or emerging technologies that can redefine modern defense strategies—before adversaries do.

Strengthening Public-Private Collaboration

Much of the DoD's innovation pipeline relies on partnerships with private contractors, startups, and academic institutions. However, these partners are also grappling with the same skills shortages in critical areas.

By investing in workforce development across the broader defense ecosystem—including vocational training, apprenticeships, and STEM education programs—the DoD can help ensure a consistent, capable flow of talent. This not only strengthens collaboration but also fosters a more agile and responsive innovation environment.

Building a Future-Ready Workforce

Bridging the skills gap isn't just about filling vacancies today—it's about preparing for the threats and challenges of tomorrow. As warfare becomes more digital, autonomous, and data-driven, the defense workforce must be equally dynamic and future-ready.

Programs that upskill current personnel, transition veterans into tech roles, and attract diverse, young talent into defense careers are vital. They help the DoD stay resilient, adaptable, and innovative in an era of rapid change.

Conclusion

Innovation is the cornerstone of U.S. military superiority, and a skilled workforce is the engine that drives it. Bridging the skills gap in the Department of Defense is not merely a workforce development issue—it is a strategic imperative. By investing in the talent needed to design, build, and deploy next-generation defense technologies, the U.S. can maintain its global edge, enhance national security, and lead the world in military innovation for decades to come.

Chapter Thirty-Three

Maintenance and Repair

T he readiness and reliability of the U.S. military depend heavily on one critical function: maintenance and repair. From aircraft and naval vessels to ground vehicles, weapons systems, and communications infrastructure, the Department of Defense (DoD) operates some of the most complex and technologically advanced equipment in the world. To keep these systems mission-ready, day in and day out, a skilled maintenance and repair workforce is essential.

However, the DoD is facing a growing skills gap—an increasing shortage of qualified technicians and mechanics with the training, experience, and certifications needed to maintain modern military equipment. Bridging this gap is not just a matter of efficiency; It is a matter of national security. A fully staffed and well-trained maintenance workforce ensures operational readiness, reduces downtime, lowers costs, and ultimately saves lives.

Enhancing Mission Readiness

Bridging the skills gap directly improves mission readiness across the armed services. Skilled maintainers can diagnose and repair issues more quickly, perform routine inspections accurately, and implement preventive maintenance that keeps equipment in peak condition. This reduces unplanned downtime and ensures that military units have the tools they need when they need them.

In a high-stakes environment where timing and reliability can make the difference between success and failure, efficient and timely maintenance is not optional—it is mission-critical.

Supporting Modernization Efforts

The DoD is undergoing a major transformation, investing in next-generation technologies such as autonomous systems, AI-powered platforms, hypersonics, and advanced communication systems. These systems require a workforce with new technical proficiencies in software, data integration, and digital troubleshooting.

Bridging the skills gap involves modernizing training programs to equip maintainers with the knowledge to support these innovations. This includes incorporating advanced diagnostic tools, augmented reality for training, and cybersecurity awareness into the skillset of military and civilian technicians.

By doing so, the DoD ensures new technologies don't become a liability because of a lack of support and that maintenance teams are prepared to manage both legacy and emerging systems.

Reducing Costs and Increasing Efficiency

Skilled maintenance personnel not only keep equipment running—they do it more cost-effectively. Properly trained technicians are less likely to misdiagnose issues, replace unnecessary parts, or perform repairs that fail to meet technical standards. This efficiency reduces wasted resources and extends the lifecycle of expensive equipment.

Additionally, improved maintenance practices reduce reliance on emergency repairs and unscheduled overhauls, which are typically more expensive and time-consuming than preventive and routine maintenance.

Strengthening the Workforce Pipeline

To bridge the gap, the DoD is increasingly partnering with technical schools, community colleges, and apprenticeship programs to build a pipeline of skilled workers. Veteran transition programs also play a key role in reskilling service members for civilian maintenance roles within defense operations.

Expanding access to these pathways ensures that a new generation of technicians is ready to take on the developing challenges of defense maintenance, both on the battlefield and at home.

Conclusion

Maintenance and repair are foundational to military strength. Without a skilled and ready workforce to support defense systems, even the most advanced technologies become liabilities. Bridging the skills gap in maintenance and repair ensures that the U.S. Department of Defense can maintain mission readiness, support modernization, reduce costs, and protect national security. Investing in people—and their skills—is one of the most strategic moves the DoD can make to sustain its operational edge.

Chapter Thirty-Four

IT Infrastructure

I n the modern era of warfare, information is power—and that power flows through complex, interconnected IT infrastructure. From global communications networks and secure data systems to cybersecurity operations and cloud computing environments, the U.S. Department of Defense (DoD) relies heavily on information technology to plan, operate, and defend its missions. As digital systems become more sophisticated, the demand for skilled IT professionals continues to rise. However, the DoD is facing a critical challenge: a growing skills gap in its IT workforce.

Bridging this skills gap is essential to strengthening and securing the DoD's IT infrastructure. Without enough qualified personnel to manage and defend its networks, maintain critical systems, and implement emerging technologies, the department risks falling behind adversaries, experiencing system vulnerabilities, and compromising national security.

Safeguarding National Security Through Cyber Readiness

Cybersecurity is a cornerstone of IT infrastructure in the defense sector. The DoD faces constant threats from nation-state actors, criminal organizations, and cyberterrorists seeking to infiltrate networks, steal classified information, or disrupt operations. Skilled IT professionals are needed to design and implement secure systems, monitor networks in real time, and respond rapidly to incidents.

Bridging the IT skills gap helps the DoD build cyber resilience. With a fully staffed and highly trained cyber workforce, the department can detect and neutralize threats before they cause damage. It also ensures better enforcement of cyber hygiene practices, more efficient patch management, and greater coordination between military and intelligence agencies.

Without the right personnel in place, even the most advanced cybersecurity tools cannot be used to their full potential. Bridging the gap gives the DoD the human resources it needs to protect sensitive information and mission-critical systems.

Enabling Digital Transformation and Innovation

The DoD is undergoing a massive digital transformation, shifting from legacy systems to modern, cloud-based, and AI-powered solutions. This transformation is essential for improving operational efficiency, enabling data-driven decision-making, and maintaining technological superiority over global adversaries.

However, digital transformation requires a skilled workforce capable of implementing, managing, and scaling these new technologies. Bridging the skills gap ensures that IT professionals within the DoD can deploy cloud services, automate workflows, integrate artificial intelligence, and optimize network performance without compromising security or reliability.

Skilled workers also help avoid costly delays or misconfigurations that can result from inadequate training or experience. With the right talent, the DoD can accelerate innovation and stay ahead in the digital domain.

Improving System Reliability and Operational Readiness

A strong IT infrastructure is not just about speed and innovation—it's about reliability. Mission readiness depends on having fully functional, secure, and responsive systems. Whether it's battlefield communications, logistics platforms, or satellite navigation, IT must work seamlessly 24/7.

Bridging the IT skills gap helps ensure these systems are properly maintained, monitored, and updated. Skilled administrators and engineers can proactively identify and resolve issues, reduce system downtime, and enhance the overall performance of digital infrastructure.

This reliability translates into faster response times, more effective operations, and a stronger strategic posture.

Building a Future-Ready Workforce

To close the IT skills gap, the DoD must continue to invest in workforce development programs—partnering with universities, expanding cyber training academies, supporting veteran transition initiatives, and modernizing internal training pathways. These efforts not only fill immediate needs but also prepare the department for future technological challenges.

Conclusion

Bridging the IT skills gap is a strategic imperative for the U.S. Department of Defense. A strong, secure, and innovative IT infrastructure underpins every aspect of modern defense operations. By investing in talent, the DoD strengthens its cyber defenses, enhances operational readiness, accelerates digital transformation, and ensures national security in an increasingly digital world.

Chapter Thirty-Five

Manufacturing

D efense-related manufacturing is a cornerstone of the U.S. Department of Defense (DoD), enabling the production of critical military equipment, advanced weapons systems, and components necessary for national defense. From aircraft and naval vessels to precision munitions and communications hardware, the ability to manufacture these systems quickly, efficiently, and at scale is essential to maintaining military readiness and strategic superiority. However, a growing skills gap in the manufacturing workforce is threatening this capability.

Bridging the skills gap is essential to strengthening the U.S. defense industrial base. Without enough qualified workers to operate advanced machinery, perform precision tasks, and manage complex production lines, the DoD risks delays in procurement, higher costs, reduced innovation, and compromised national security. Addressing this challenge ensures that America's defense manufacturing capabilities remain agile, modern, and globally competitive.

Enhancing Production Speed and Readiness

Bridging the skills gap directly improves the DoD's ability to produce defense systems on time and on budget. Skilled manufacturing workers can efficiently operate equipment, interpret technical blueprints, and adapt quickly to changing production demands. Their expertise reduces the likelihood of errors, rework, and quality control issues that can delay delivery timelines and strain supply chains.

Faster, more reliable production supports the military's readiness goals. In times of conflict or crisis, the ability to ramp up production of critical systems—from armored vehicles to ammunition—is essential. A well-trained workforce enables the defense industrial base to respond rapidly and effectively, providing warfighters with the tools they need to succeed.

Supporting Advanced Manufacturing and Innovation

Modern defense manufacturing is undergoing a transformation, driven by new technologies such as digital design, automation, artificial intelligence, and advanced materials. These innovations offer powerful advantages: reduced production time, lower costs, improved performance, and greater customization. However, leveraging them requires a workforce with updated skills in Computer-Aided Design (CAD), robotics programming, data analysis, and other high-tech disciplines.

Bridging the skills gap means equipping workers with these capabilities. Training programs, apprenticeships, and partnerships with technical colleges and universities can prepare workers for the developing needs of defense manufacturers. A skilled workforce is more capable of supporting research and development efforts, bringing innovative ideas from the lab to the production floor, and integrating emerging technologies into defense systems.

Strengthening Supply Chain Resilience

Defense manufacturing is not confined to a single plant or facility—it is part of a complex, interconnected supply chain involving thousands of contractors and suppliers. When there are workforce shortages in any part of this chain, it creates bottlenecks that affect the entire system.

Bridging the skills gap helps build a more resilient and responsive supply chain. Skilled workers ensure that every link in the chain—from small component suppliers to final assembly lines—can meet DoD requirements efficiently and reliably. This resilience is especially important in a world of increasing geopolitical tensions and supply chain disruptions.

Conclusion

The strength of the U.S. military depends not only on its soldiers and strategies but also on its ability to build and sustain the equipment they use. Bridging the skills gap in defense-related manufacturing is a national priority. It ensures timely production, supports technological innovation, strengthens supply chains, and maintains America's strategic advantage on the global stage. By investing in workforce development and training, the Department of Defense can secure the industrial capabilities that are essential to protecting the nation—today and into the future.

Section 6: 8 Ways to Bridge the Skills Gap

Chapter Thirty-Six

Conduct a Skills Gap Analysis

I n today's rapidly evolving workforce landscape, organizations must be agile, innovative, and forward-thinking to stay competitive. Whether it's due to emerging technologies, shifting industry standards, or changing customer demands, the skills required to succeed are constantly changing. One of the most effective tools for addressing these changes and preparing a future-ready workforce is the skills gap analysis.

A skills gap analysis is the process of comparing the current skills of employees to the skills required to meet business objectives. It identifies where gaps exist and helps organizations make strategic decisions about training, hiring, and development. Far from being just an HR exercise, a skills gap analysis is a critical component of long-term organizational success.

Aligning Workforce Capabilities With Business Goals

The most immediate benefit of conducting a skills gap analysis is ensuring that your workforce is equipped to meet organizational goals. Companies often create ambitious strategic plans without evaluating whether their teams have the skills to execute them. A skills gap analysis helps bridge this disconnect by aligning talent capabilities with business needs.

For example, if a manufacturing company plans to implement a new automated system, it must ensure that employees are trained in automation and digital tools. Without the necessary skills in place, the transition could lead to inefficiencies, delays, or costly errors. A skills gap analysis identifies this need in advance, allowing the organization to plan accordingly.

Improving Training and Workforce Development

Once skill gaps are identified, organizations can take a targeted approach to workforce development. Instead of offering generic training programs, a skills gap analysis allows businesses to design learning and development initiatives that directly address the areas where improvement is most needed.

This leads to better outcomes and a higher return on investment. Employees receive training that is relevant to their roles, increasing engagement and retention, while the organization benefits from a more capable and confident workforce.

Additionally, a skills gap analysis supports succession planning by highlighting where potential future leaders may need additional training or experience to be ready for advancement.

Enhancing Recruitment and Talent Acquisition

In many cases, skill gaps cannot be filled through training alone—especially when time is limited or specialized expertise is required. A skills gap analysis can inform recruitment strategies by identifying exactly what skills are missing and where new talent is needed.

This clarity allows HR teams to create more accurate job descriptions, ask better interview questions, and prioritize candidates who bring the necessary competencies. It also helps in reducing hiring bias by focusing on objective skill needs rather than vague qualifications.

Moreover, a clear understanding of internal skill gaps can help companies make smarter decisions about outsourcing, contract work, or partnerships when hiring is not the best option.

Staying Competitive in a Rapidly Changing Market

In an era defined by digital transformation, automation, and global competition, businesses that fail to adapt quickly fall behind. A skills gap analysis enables organizations to stay proactive rather than reactive. By regularly assessing skill levels and forecasting future needs, companies can evolve with their industries instead of scrambling to catch up.

This forward-thinking approach not only boosts internal performance but also strengthens a company's reputation in the marketplace. Customers, partners, and investors are more likely to trust organizations that are continuously improving and investing in their people.

Boosting Employee Engagement and Retention

Employees want to grow in their roles and feel confident about their future. A skills gap analysis sends a clear message: the organization cares about its people and is committed to their professional development.

By identifying skill gaps and offering training or new opportunities, companies empower employees to take charge of their growth. This boosts morale, improves job satisfaction, and reduces turnover—key components of a strong and sustainable workforce.

Conclusion

A skills gap analysis is more than just a diagnostic tool—it's a strategic asset. It helps align talent with business goals, improves training effectiveness, sharpens recruitment efforts, and positions organizations for long-term success. In a world of constant change, companies that take the time to understand and address their skill gaps will be the ones that innovate, grow, and lead the way into the future.

Chapter Thirty-Seven

Change the Messaging

The skills gap in the United States is one of the most pressing challenges facing the modern workforce. Thousands of high-paying jobs in manufacturing, skilled trades, healthcare, IT, and other technical fields remain unfilled—not because these jobs don't exist, but because too few people are pursuing the training needed to do them. While workforce development programs and education reform are vital parts of the solution, one often overlooked but equally crucial piece is messaging—specifically, how advertising and marketing shape public perception of work and career pathways.

If we want to close the skills gap in America, we must first change the narrative. For decades, advertising, media, and cultural messaging have defined success as a four-year college degree leading to a white-collar job. Meanwhile, careers in trades and technical fields have been largely underrepresented, or worse, stigmatized. This messaging has not only influenced individual career choices—it has fueled a national workforce imbalance that threatens our economy and competitiveness.

Redefining Success

The traditional notion that success only comes with a bachelor's degree has been drilled into generations of students, parents, and educators. As a result, millions of young people have pursued college degrees—often accumulating debt—without a clear career path, while high-demand skilled careers go unnoticed.

Advertising and marketing play a powerful role in shaping perceptions. To fix the skills gap, we need to rebrand what it means to be successful. Messaging should highlight the value of hands-on, technical work and emphasize that skilled trades offer not only good pay but also stability, purpose, innovation, and opportunities for advancement. Campaigns must showcase real people thriving in careers like welding, CNC machining, plumbing, IT support, and advanced manufacturing—not as a fallback option, but as a smart and fulfilling first choice.

Telling a New Story

People are inspired by stories, not statistics. That's why marketing efforts to close the skills gap must go beyond promoting training programs—they must tell compelling stories about the people behind the tools, machines, and technologies that drive our economy.

By featuring diverse, relatable workers and apprentices in these roles, marketing can challenge outdated stereotypes and appeal to a broader audience. These stories can be told through social media campaigns, video content, community events, influencer partnerships, and national advertising efforts. When individuals see people like themselves building successful careers in skilled fields, they're more likely to see those paths as viable and valuable.

Emphasizing Modern Technology and Innovation

Another key messaging shift is to highlight the technology-driven nature of modern trades and manufacturing. Many people still associate these jobs with outdated images of dirty, monotonous labor. In reality, today's manufacturing floors and skilled trades environments are filled with advanced technologies—automation, robotics, 3D printing, and smart machine systems.

Marketing must reframe these roles as high-tech, innovative, and future-focused. This is particularly important for reaching younger generations, who are naturally drawn to technology and may not realize that careers in trades and tech often overlap. By showing how these careers are both intellectually and technologically engaging, we can attract more interest and enthusiasm.

Reaching the Right Audience

To make the biggest impact, marketing messages need to be targeted and strategic. High school students, career changers, military veterans, and underemployed workers are all potential candidates for skilled careers—but each group requires a tailored message. Partnerships with schools, community organizations, workforce development organizations, and employers can help ensure the message reaches the people who need to hear it most.

A Collaborative Effort

Fixing the messaging around skilled careers requires collaboration. Industry leaders, educators, public agencies, media professionals, and marketers must work together to reshape how America views work, education, and opportunity. The message should be clear: skilled careers are not second-tier—they are essential, rewarding, and open to everyone.

Conclusion

The skills gap is not just an economic issue—it's a storytelling issue. By changing the way we talk about work, careers, and success, we can inspire a new generation of workers to pursue the high-demand roles that keep our country running. Effective advertising and marketing have the power to shift perceptions, elevate skilled careers, and help close the skills gap—for good.

Chapter Thirty-Eight

Upskilling and Reskilling

T he U.S. workforce is at a crossroads. While millions of jobs go unfilled across industries such as manufacturing, healthcare, information technology, logistics, and skilled trades, many workers are either unemployed or underemployed. This paradox highlights a growing challenge: the skills gap—the disconnect between the skills employers need and the skills the current workforce possesses.

To close this gap and prepare for the future of work, the United States must prioritize upskilling and reskilling. These strategies are not just buzzwords—they are vital tools for economic growth, workforce sustainability, and global competitiveness. By helping workers gain new or improved skills, we can align talent with opportunity and build a more resilient, adaptable economy.

Understanding Upskilling and Reskilling

Upskilling involves teaching employees new skills to help them grow in their current roles or take on more advanced responsibilities. For example, a machine operator might learn how to program a CNC machine or interpret data from smart sensors to optimize performance.

Reskilling, on the other hand, prepares workers for entirely new roles, often in different fields. This is essential for individuals whose jobs are being phased out due to automation, digital transformation, or shifting industry demands. For instance, a retail worker might be reskilled for a career in IT support or advanced manufacturing.

Both upskilling and reskilling help workers remain relevant in a labor market that is constantly evolving.

Responding to Technological Change

Technological advancement is one of the key drivers of the skills gap. As automation, artificial intelligence, and digital tools become more prevalent, job roles are changing rapidly. While some jobs are disappearing, others are emerging, and nearly all are becoming more complex and tech-dependent.

To keep up, workers must continuously learn and adapt. Upskilling ensures that employees can work alongside new technologies rather than be replaced by them. Reskilling offers a lifeline to displaced workers, helping them transition into high-demand, future-focused careers.

Failing to act risks leaving millions of Americans behind and creating talent shortages that stifle business growth and innovation.

Supporting Economic Growth and Competitiveness

A skilled workforce is the foundation of a robust economy. Companies cannot expand, innovate, or deliver quality services without qualified employees. Yet, according to recent reports, the U.S. could face millions of unfilled jobs over the next decade because of a lack of skilled labor.

Upskilling and reskilling can reverse this trend by preparing workers for in-demand jobs. This, in turn, boosts productivity, reduces unemployment, and strengthens the nation's position in the global economy. Countries that invest in workforce development are better positioned to attract investment, build strong supply chains, and lead in emerging industries like clean energy, biotechnology, and advanced manufacturing.

Empowering Workers and Strengthening Communities

Beyond economics, upskilling and reskilling have a profound impact on people's lives. They provide pathways to better-paying jobs, increased job security, and personal fulfillment. Workers gain confidence, employers benefit from greater engagement and retention, and communities become more stable and prosperous.

Programs that target underserved populations—including women, minorities, veterans, and displaced workers—help create a more diverse and robust workforce. When more people have access to training and opportunity, everyone benefits.

A Collaborative Effort

Fixing the skills gap through upskilling and reskilling requires collaboration across sectors. Employers must invest in training programs and create clear career pathways. Educators and workforce development organizations must design flexible, relevant curricula. Government agencies must provide funding, incentives, and infrastructure to support lifelong learning.

Public-private partnerships, apprenticeships, industry-led credential programs, and online learning platforms are all part of the solution. Together, these initiatives can create a national ecosystem of continuous learning.

Conclusion

The skills gap is not a future problem—it's a current crisis. But it's also an opportunity. By embracing upskilling and reskilling, the United States can empower its workforce, fuel economic growth, and secure a more competitive future. The path forward is clear: invest in people, invest in skills, and invest in the future of work.

Chapter Thirty-Nine

Coaching and Mentoring

C oaching and mentoring provide workers with direct, hands-on guidance and support from experienced professionals. These relationships can accelerate learning, improve retention of knowledge, and boost confidence—making them invaluable tools for developing talent and closing the skills gap. As industries continue to evolve, coaching and mentoring will play a key role in preparing the workforce for both today's jobs and tomorrow's challenges.

The Power of Mentorship

Mentorship connects less-experienced individuals (mentees) with seasoned professionals (mentors) who offer guidance, encouragement, and insights. This relationship fosters not just technical learning but also professional development, helping mentees navigate their careers with greater clarity and confidence.

In the context of addressing the skills gap, mentors can help newcomers understand complex job functions, company-specific procedures, and industry expectations. They also pass down tacit knowledge—those unwritten rules and best practices that aren't found in training manuals or standard operating procedure papers.

Mentorship is especially important for younger workers entering skilled trades, tech fields, or manufacturing, where experience and hands-on learning are key. It's also valuable for career changers and individuals reentering the workforce, who may need extra support to adapt to new roles or technologies.

The Role of Coaching in Skills Development

Coaching takes a more performance-oriented approach, often focused on helping individuals improve specific skills or overcome challenges in real time. Coaches—whether managers, trainers, or dedicated professionals—work closely with employees to assess strengths, identify gaps, set goals, and provide ongoing feedback.

In industries facing rapid technological change, coaching helps employees stay current and continuously improve. For example, a technician learning to use a new digital diagnostic tool may benefit from a coach who provides hands-on demonstrations, immediate feedback, and troubleshooting support.

Coaching also helps cultivate soft skills—such as communication, teamwork, and leadership—which are increasingly valued by employers but are difficult to teach in traditional classroom settings.

Strengthening Employer Engagement and Retention

For employers, investing in coaching and mentoring programs leads to higher retention, stronger employee engagement, and a more agile workforce. Employees who feel supported and connected to mentors or coaches are more likely to stay with their organizations and continue growing within them.

Companies that embed mentoring into onboarding, training, and career development can more effectively transfer institutional knowledge and prepare workers for leadership roles. This creates a sustainable talent pipeline and reduces the cost and disruption of turnover.

Conclusion

To truly fix the skills gap in the United States, we need more than just education—we need connection. Coaching and mentoring offer the personal guidance and real-world insight that no textbook can provide. By supporting workers through one-on-one relationships, we can speed up learning, build confidence, and unlock potential across the American workforce. In a time of rapid change and growing demand, coaching and mentoring aren't optional—they're essential.

Chapter Forty

Hands-On Authentic Learning

To effectively close the skills gap, we must embrace hands-on and authentic learning as core strategies for developing real-world skills. Authentic, experiential learning connects education to industry by giving learners opportunities to apply knowledge in real-world settings. It transforms abstract concepts into tangible skills and builds confidence through practice. Whether it's through apprenticeships, internships, lab work, maker spaces, or project-based learning, hands-on experiences are essential to preparing a workforce that's ready to contribute on day one.

Bridging the Gap Between Theory and Practice

One of the biggest shortcomings in traditional education is the disconnect between what students learn in the classroom and what they need to succeed in the workplace. Many graduates leave school with theoretical knowledge but lack the ability to apply it in practical settings. This is especially true in technical fields that require operational, mechanical, or digital skills.

Hands-on learning bridges this gap by providing opportunities to practice using real tools, solve real problems, and navigate real work environments. For example, a student learning advanced manufacturing can operate CNC machines in a training lab or during an apprenticeship, rather than just reading about machining in a textbook. This kind of experience builds muscle memory, decision-making skills, and confidence.

Preparing Students for In-Demand Careers

Authentic learning allows students to explore career paths in high-demand industries and gain the skills employers are looking for. Whether it's welding, software development, nursing, or solar panel installation, these roles require more than just academic understanding—they demand hands-on competence.

Through programs like career and technical education (CTE), students can gain certifications, earn college credits, and even start working in their chosen fields while still in high school. This fast-track approach not only accelerates entry into the workforce but also helps address labor shortages in essential sectors.

Furthermore, exposing students early to skilled professions helps combat outdated stereotypes about the trades and technical careers, promoting them as smart, rewarding alternatives to traditional four-year degrees.

Building Critical Soft Skills

Besides technical expertise, employers consistently emphasize the importance of soft skills—communication, teamwork, adaptability, and problem-solving. These are difficult to teach in a lecture-based classroom but are naturally developed through hands-on learning experiences.

When students work in teams to complete a project, troubleshoot a machine, or deliver a real-world solution to a business partner, they're building these soft skills in context. These experiences simulate the dynamics of the workplace and better prepare students for professional success.

Supporting Underserved Communities

Authentic learning also plays a key role in supporting equity in education and workforce development. Many students—particularly in underserved or marginalized communities—benefit more from experiential, applied learning than from traditional academic models.

By giving all learners access to real-world training, internships, and industry-connected experiences, we create a more inclusive pathway to high-quality jobs. Hands-on learning can be a powerful equalizer, offering practical routes to success without requiring a four-year degree.

Encouraging Lifelong Learning and Adaptability

The nature of work is constantly evolving, and hands-on learning prepares individuals to be lifelong learners. When people are trained to learn by doing, they are more adaptable and capable of acquiring new skills throughout their careers. This agility is essential in a fast-changing economy and helps future-proof the workforce.

Conclusion

To close the skills gap in the United States, we need to rethink how we prepare people for work. Hands-on and authentic learning is not just an alternative—it's a necessity. By giving learners actual experiences, practical skills, and meaningful exposure to the working world, we empower them to step into high-demand careers with confidence and competence. Bridging the gap between education and employment starts with rolling up our sleeves and learning by doing.

Chapter Forty-One

Licensures and Certifications

A mericans seek better job opportunities. One key solution to this problem lies in expanding access to licensures, credentials, and certifications that validate real-world skills and bridge the gap between education and employment. These credentials are essential tools for ensuring that workers have the knowledge, training, and abilities needed to perform specific jobs. When widely recognized and aligned with industry standards, they offer a pathway for both new entrants to the workforce and existing workers looking to upskill or reskill. In short, licensures, credentials, and certifications are powerful instruments for closing the skills gap and strengthening the U.S. labor force.

Defining the Value of Credentials

Licensures, credentials, and certifications each serve a distinct purpose:

- Licensures are legally required qualifications to perform certain regulated occupations (e.g., electricians, nurses, plumbers). They ensure public safety and uphold professional standards.

- Certifications are industry-recognized validations of specific skills or knowledge, such as CompTIA for IT, AWS certification for cloud computing, or Smart Automation Certification Alliance (SACA) for micro-credentialing across a wide variety of industrially relevant core competencies.

- Credentials is a broader term that can include diplomas, certificates, badges, or degrees, showing completion of a training program or educational achievement.

Together, these credentials provide clear, measurable proof of competency. For employers, they reduce the guesswork in hiring by verifying that a candidate meets industry-defined standards. For workers, they offer credibility, mobility, and access to better job opportunities.

Fast-Tracking Employment and Career Growth

One of the biggest advantages of industry certifications and credentials is that they can be earned more quickly and affordably than a traditional four-year degree. Many in-demand fields—such as cybersecurity, welding, HVAC repair, and medical assisting—require specific skills that can be acquired through short-term training and validated through certification.

This makes credentials particularly valuable for career changes, recent high school graduates, and displaced workers who need a fast path into a high-demand career. By expanding access to credentialing programs through community colleges, trade schools, apprenticeships, and online platforms, we can quickly equip more Americans with the skills employers are actively seeking.

Aligning Education with Industry Needs

Too often, traditional education programs are not aligned with the real-time needs of employers. Certifications and credentials, on the other hand, are usually developed with direct input from industry leaders, making them more responsive to labor market demands.

When employers and educators work together to develop and promote credentialing pathways, they create a more agile and relevant training ecosystem. This ensures that job seekers are learning the right skills and that employers can find talent ready to contribute on day one.

Promoting Lifelong Learning and Upskilling

As technology continues to transform the workplace, lifelong learning is essential. Certifications provide a practical way for workers to stay current with new tools, technologies, and practices. Earning a new credential can help a worker advance within their current company, switch industries, or gain a competitive edge in the job market.

Stackable credentials—short-term, incremental certifications that build toward larger qualifications—are especially effective. They allow individuals to learn in phases, gain confidence, and move forward in their careers without committing to several years of full-time education.

Conclusion

Fixing the skills gap in the U.S. isn't just about creating more jobs—it's about preparing more people to do them well. Licensures, credentials, and certifications provide a trusted, scalable way to connect workers with opportunity and employers with talent. As industries evolve and the demand for skilled labor grows, these tools will be essential to building a competitive, inclusive, and future-ready workforce.

Chapter Forty-Two

Leveraging Technology

The United States is grappling with a significant skills gap—millions of jobs remain unfilled because of a lack of qualified workers, even as many Americans search for meaningful employment. This disconnect poses a serious threat to economic growth, industry competitiveness, and workforce mobility. But amid the challenge lies an opportunity: technology. With the right tools and strategic use of digital innovation, technology can help close the skills gap by making education more accessible, training more effective, and career pathways more visible and inclusive.

The Current Landscape

The skills gap is particularly pronounced in industries like advanced manufacturing, cybersecurity, healthcare, logistics, and the skilled trades. Employers struggle to find workers with the right mix of technical, digital, and soft skills, while workers often lack access to the training and resources needed to fill these roles.

At the same time, the pace of technological change is accelerating. New jobs are emerging that require up-to-date knowledge in areas like artificial intelligence, data analytics, robotics, and cloud computing. Traditional methods of training and education alone cannot keep up—but technology can help bridge the gap faster and more efficiently.

Online Learning and Microcredentials

One of the most impactful ways technology is helping to close the skills gap is through online learning platforms. From community colleges to global ed-tech companies, digital learning environments are offering flexible, affordable, and personalized education.

Online courses, microcredentials, and certifications allow learners to gain specific, job-relevant skills at their own pace, often without the time or cost of a traditional degree. Platforms like Coursera, edX, LinkedIn Learning, and others partner with industry leaders to offer high-quality training for in-demand areas such as IT support, project management, welding, and digital marketing.

By embracing online education, more Americans—especially working adults, rural populations, and underserved communities—can gain the skills needed to fill open jobs.

Virtual Reality (VR) and Augmented Reality (AR) Training

Emerging technologies like Virtual Reality (VR) and Augmented Reality (AR) are transforming how hands-on skills are taught. In fields such as construction, manufacturing, and healthcare, VR and AR simulations allow learners to practice real-world scenarios in a safe and controlled environment.

For example, a technician can learn how to repair a turbine or operate complex machinery through immersive simulations before stepping onto the factory floor. This not only improves retention and confidence but also reduces training costs and safety risks.

As these technologies become more affordable and scalable, they offer a game-changing way to train workers at scale for high-stakes, high-skill roles.

AI-Powered Career Pathways and Skills Matching

Artificial Intelligence (AI) is another powerful tool in addressing the skills gap. AI-powered platforms can analyze labor market data to identify in-demand jobs, recommend relevant training, and match workers to positions based on their existing skills and experience.

For job seekers, these tools provide clear pathways for advancement, helping them understand what skills they need to acquire and where they can find training. For employers, AI can help streamline recruitment by identifying candidates with the most potential—even those without traditional credentials.

This kind of intelligent skills mapping makes the training process more efficient and ensures that both workers and businesses are aligned with the needs of a dynamic economy.

Conclusion

The skills gap is a complex and urgent problem—but it's also an opportunity to rethink how we prepare people for the jobs of tomorrow. Technology is not a silver bullet, but it is a powerful enabler. From online learning and immersive training to AI-driven career guidance, technology offers scalable, accessible, and effective solutions to help the U.S. build a future-ready workforce. By embracing these tools, we can close the skills gap and create a stronger, more inclusive economy for all.

Chapter Forty-Three

Cloud-Based Learning

W hile there's no single solution to the complex problem of the ever-widening skills gap in the United States, one powerful and scalable tool stands out: cloud-based learning. As the demand for flexible, accessible, and industry-aligned education continues to rise, cloud-based learning platforms are emerging as a vital force in reshaping workforce development and closing the skills gap.

What Is Cloud-Based Learning?

Cloud-based learning refers to educational content and resources delivered through the internet via cloud computing technology. Learners can access training materials, video lessons, assessments, simulations, and collaboration tools from any device at any time. Unlike traditional in-person training, cloud-based platforms offer flexibility and scale, making it easier for individuals and organizations to access and deliver skills-based education.

Popular examples of cloud-based learning platforms include Coursera, edX, Khan Academy, Google Cloud Skills Boost, LinkedIn Learning, and industry-specific portals developed by companies and trade associations.

Flexibility for Today's Learners

One of the biggest barriers to skills training is time. Many working adults, parents, or those with multiple jobs simply cannot attend in-person classes or commit to full-time programs. Cloud-based learning solves this problem by offering anytime, anywhere access to self-directed educational content.

This flexibility makes training accessible to a broader segment of the population—especially those who are balancing work, caregiving, or geographic limitations. Whether someone is learning after hours, on weekends, or during breaks at work, cloud-based platforms make it possible to build skills on their schedule.

Rapid Response to Industry Needs

Another key benefit of cloud-based learning is its ability to quickly adapt to changing workforce demands. Unlike traditional academic institutions that may take months or years to update curricula, cloud-based platforms can rapidly release new courses based on emerging skills, industry trends, or technological shifts.

For example, if a surge in demand occurs for cloud computing professionals, cybersecurity analysts, or CNC machine operators, cloud-based learning platforms can quickly roll out targeted training programs aligned with real-world job requirements. This agile approach ensures that learners are gaining relevant, up-to-date skills that translate directly into employment opportunities.

Scalable Solutions for Employers

Employers play a critical role in closing the skills gap, and cloud-based learning offers them a scalable, cost-effective solution to train current employees. Companies can use these platforms to reskill and upskill workers without pulling them away from their jobs for extended periods.

With cloud-based dashboards, managers can track employee progress, assess performance, and customize learning pathways. This makes internal workforce development more measurable and strategic. It also helps businesses stay competitive by building the talent they need from within.

A Foundation for Lifelong Learning

As the job market continues to evolve, lifelong learning will be essential. Cloud-based platforms support continuous skill development through microlearning, stackable credentials, and modular courses. Learners can build knowledge incrementally and adjust their learning path based on career goals and job market trends.

This ongoing, self-directed learning model is exactly what the modern economy demands—and cloud-based learning makes it both possible and practical.

Conclusion

The skills gap is a national challenge, but it's also a tremendous opportunity to reimagine how we prepare people for meaningful work. Cloud-based learning offers a flexible, scalable, and inclusive way to deliver the skills training America needs—when, where, and how learners need it. By embracing this technology, we can connect more people to opportunity, empower employers to build talent from within, and help close the skills gap for good.

Section 7: 7-Step Skills Gap Analysis

Chapter Forty-Four

Define Your Business Goals

E stablishing clear, strategic business goals is essential for guiding your company's direction, measuring success, and aligning your team's efforts. Without well-defined goals, even the most passionate business owners can lose focus, misallocate resources, and struggle to grow. Whether you're launching a startup or scaling an established company, setting the right goals helps you stay intentional and on track.

Here's a step-by-step guide to help you establish business goals that are realistic, actionable, and aligned with your long-term vision.

Define Your Vision and Mission

Before setting specific goals, you need a clear understanding of your business's purpose and direction.

- Vision: What do you ultimately want your business to achieve?

- Mission: Why does your business exist? What value does it offer customers?

Your vision and mission provide the foundation for your goals. Every goal you set should support and move you closer to your overall vision.

Example:

- Vision: "To become the most trusted local organic food provider in our region."

- Mission: "To deliver fresh, healthy, and sustainable food options to our community."

Conduct a SWOT Analysis

A SWOT analysis (Strengths, Weaknesses, Opportunities, Threats) helps you understand where your business currently stands and what factors could affect its goals. It provides the context you need to set realistic and strategic objectives.

- Strengths: What are you doing well?

- Weaknesses: What areas need improvement?

- Opportunities: What market trends or gaps can you take advantage of?

- Threats: What external challenges could hinder your progress?

Use this analysis to identify areas where goal-setting can lead to meaningful improvement or innovation.

Identify Your Key Business Areas

Next, pinpoint the core areas of your business that need focused goals. Common areas include:

- Sales and revenue

- Marketing and customer engagement

- Product or service development

- Customer service and satisfaction

- Operations and efficiency

- Human resources and team development

- Financial management

Establishing goals for each of these key areas ensures a balanced and comprehensive approach to growth.

Conclusion

Establishing business goals is one of the most powerful things you can do to drive clarity, performance, and long-term success. By following a structured, step-by-step approach—from defining your vision to measuring your progress—you create a roadmap that keeps your business focused, your team aligned, and your future bright. Strategic goals aren't just tasks on a to-do list—they're the building blocks of your business's legacy.

Chapter Forty-Five

Identify the Skills Required

I n any business, success depends heavily on having the right people in the right roles with the right skills. Whether you're hiring new employees, restructuring a team, or planning for growth, understanding the specific skills each role requires is essential. Clearly defining these skills helps align hiring practices, streamline training programs, and ensure everyone is equipped to contribute effectively to your organization's goals.

Here's a step-by-step guide on how to identify the skills required for each role within your business.

Start With a Clear Job Description

Begin by writing or reviewing the job description for each role. A well-crafted job description outlines the principal duties, responsibilities, and expectations of the position. It serves as a foundational document from which skill requirements can be identified.

Ask yourself:

- What are the core responsibilities of this role?

- What tasks will the employee perform daily, weekly, or monthly?

- What tools, systems, or processes will they use?

The answers to these questions will point you toward the essential skills the role demands.

Break Down Skills into Categories

To identify the full scope of necessary skills, it's helpful to divide them into three key categories:

- Technical Skills (Hard Skills): These are job-specific abilities, such as proficiency in software, equipment operation, data analysis, or accounting. They're often measurable and teachable.

- Soft Skills (Interpersonal Skills): These include communication, teamwork, time management, adaptability, and problem-solving. While harder to quantify, soft skills are just as important, especially for roles involving collaboration or leadership.

- Role-Specific Knowledge: This refers to industry knowledge or understanding of specific regulations, processes, or methodologies relevant to the role, such as compliance standards or sales pipelines.

For example, a marketing manager might need hard skills in SEO and data analytics, soft skills in leadership and creativity, and role-specific knowledge of brand positioning and campaign strategies.

Consult With Managers and Team Leaders

Managers and team leaders who work closely with specific roles have first-hand knowledge of the skills needed to succeed. Schedule meetings or conduct surveys with supervisors to gather their input.

Ask them:

- What skills make top performers in this role stand out?

- What common gaps do new hires struggle with?

- Are there emerging skills that will become more important in the future?

This feedback can help you refine and prioritize the most relevant skills.

Observe and Analyze Current Employees

Another effective approach is to observe your best employees in each role. Analyze what they do well and how they approach their tasks. Often, job performance goes beyond what's written in the job description, so watching real-world behavior can uncover overlooked or underestimated skills.

You can also use performance reviews, peer feedback, and productivity metrics to identify patterns and strengths among top performers.

Research Industry Standards and Trends

Reviewing industry benchmarks and job postings from other companies can help you validate and enhance your skill requirements. Job boards, professional associations, and labor market data often reveal which skills are in demand and evolving.

Technology is changing many roles quickly, so staying updated with trends ensures your team stays competitive and future-ready.

Use Skill Assessment Tools

Consider using skills assessments and role-based evaluations to determine what competencies a job requires. These tools can also help identify skill gaps in current employees and guide training or hiring decisions.

Skills matrices, for example, allow you to map required skills against current team capabilities—giving you a visual overview of strengths and development needs.

Keep Skills Lists Updated

Roles change over time. As your business grows, new tools, challenges, and expectations will emerge. Make it a habit to review and update skill requirements regularly, especially during performance evaluations, restructuring, or hiring phases.

Conclusion

Identifying the skills required for each role is not just an HR task—it's a strategic practice that ensures your business is equipped for success. By clearly defining technical, soft, and role-specific skills and by gathering insights from multiple sources, you can create a firm foundation for recruitment, development, and long-term performance. In today's fast-changing world, knowing what each role truly requires is key to building a capable, confident, and future-ready workforce.

Chapter Forty-Six

Assess Current Employee Skills

I n today's competitive and fast-changing business landscape, having a skilled and adaptable workforce is essential for long-term success. While hiring new talent can help fill gaps, one of the most effective strategies is to understand and maximize the potential of your current employees. That begins with a clear and thorough skills assessment process.

Assessing employee skills not only helps identify strengths and development needs—it also enables better workforce planning, training investments, succession strategies, and employee engagement. Here's a step-by-step guide on how to assess the skills of current employees within your organization.

Define the Skills You Need

Before you assess what your employees can do, you need to clearly define what skills are required for success in each role and department. These skills may fall into three major categories:

- Technical Skills: Job-specific abilities, such as data analysis, coding, machine operation, or accounting.

- Soft Skills: Interpersonal attributes like communication, teamwork, adaptability, and leadership.

- Industry or Role-Specific Knowledge: Understanding of regulations, processes, tools, or methodologies unique to your field.

Use job descriptions, performance expectations, and input from team leads to create a skills framework or checklist for each role.

Use Self-Assessments

A great starting point is to ask employees to evaluate their own skills. Self-assessments promote reflection and encourage workers to take ownership of their development.

Provide them with a skills checklist tailored to their role and ask them to rate their proficiency in each area—using a simple scale (e.g., beginner, intermediate, advanced). Include open-ended questions that invite employees to identify areas they'd like to improve or learn more about.

Keep in mind that self-assessments may contain bias, so they should be paired with other evaluation methods for a complete picture.

Get Manager and Peer Feedback

Supervisors and coworkers offer valuable insight into an employee's capabilities. 360-degree feedback gathers observations from multiple sources—managers, peers, and direct reports—providing a well-rounded view of performance.

Ask managers to assess:

- How well the employee meets job expectations

- Their ability to take initiative and solve problems

- Technical competencies and collaboration skills

- Areas where the employee could grow

This type of feedback uncovers strengths that may go unnoticed and identifies areas where employees might need additional support or training.

Conduct Skills Assessments or Tests

Depending on your industry, consider using formal skills assessments to objectively measure knowledge and abilities. These can include:

- Online quizzes or simulations that test knowledge of software, processes, or tools

- Practical tasks or job simulations that demonstrate skills in a real-world scenario

- Role-playing exercises to assess communication, leadership, or sales skills

These assessments can be designed internally or sourced through third-party platforms tailored to your industry.

Use a Skills Matrix

A skills matrix is a visual tool that maps employees' skills against role requirements. It allows you to quickly identify:

- Skills that are strong across your team

- Skills that are missing or underdeveloped

- Opportunities for mentoring, cross-training, or upskilling

Each employee is listed along with their rated proficiency in relevant skills. This matrix helps leaders make informed decisions about promotions, project assignments, and training investments.

Review Performance Data

Your performance management system can offer valuable clues about an employee's skill level. Review:

- Past performance reviews

- Project outcomes

- Key performance indicators (KPIs)

- Client or customer feedback

This data helps validate other assessments and shows how effectively employees apply their skills in day-to-day work.

Follow Up With Development Plans

Once you've assessed employees' skills, the next step is to create personalized development plans. Use the results to identify:

- Training opportunities

- Career growth paths

- Stretch assignments

- Coaching or mentoring needs

Regular follow-up ensures skills stay current and aligned with evolving business goals.

Conclusion

Assessing the skills of your current employees is not just about evaluation—it's about empowerment. By taking a structured, thoughtful approach, you'll uncover hidden strengths, bridge skill gaps, and create a more agile, motivated workforce. In doing so, your organization becomes more prepared for change, more competitive in the market, and better positioned for long-term success.

Chapter Forty-Seven

Identify and Prioritize the Gaps

K nowing where your workforce falls short is the first step toward building a focused, cost-effective talent development strategy. Here's a step-by-step guide on how to identify and prioritize skills gaps within your organization.

Align Skills Assessments With Business Goals

Before diving into individual skills, it's essential to start with a clear understanding of your business objectives. What is your organization trying to achieve in the short and long term? Are you launching new products, entering new markets, increasing automation, or focusing on customer experience?

Each of these goals requires specific capabilities. By linking workforce skills to strategic objectives, you can ensure that your gap analysis focuses on what truly matters to your organization's success.

Define Required Skills for Each Role

To identify skills gaps, you must first know what skills are required. Review each role within your organization and create or update a list of necessary competencies. These should include:

- Technical skills (e.g., coding, data analysis, equipment operation)

- Soft skills (e.g., communication, leadership, adaptability)

- Role-specific knowledge (e.g., industry regulations, product expertise)

Consult job descriptions, department heads, and team leaders to ensure your skill lists reflect current responsibilities and future demands.

Conduct a Skills Inventory

Once you've defined the required skills, assess the existing skill levels of your employees. Use a combination of methods:

- Self-assessments: Employees rate their own proficiency in specific skills.

- Manager evaluations: Supervisors provide feedback on employee capabilities.

- Performance data: Review KPIs, project outcomes, and performance reviews.

- Skills assessments: Use tests, simulations, or real-world tasks to evaluate abilities.

This inventory creates a baseline that shows where each employee or team currently stands compared to the desired skill level.

Identify the Gaps

Compare your skills inventory to your list of required competencies. The difference between what is needed and what currently exists is your skills gap. These gaps can fall into several categories:

- Individual gaps: A specific employee lacks certain skills for their current role.

- Team-level gaps: A department lacks strength in a critical area.

- Organization-wide gaps: Broad deficiencies in skills that affect overall performance or growth (e.g., digital literacy, data security, project management).

Prioritize the Most Critical Gaps

Not all skills gaps are equally urgent. To prioritize, ask:

- Which gaps are hindering current operations?

- Which gaps will impact future growth or strategy?

- Which gaps pose the greatest risk (e.g., compliance, security)?

- Which gaps affect multiple employees or departments?

Rank each gap based on its business impact, urgency, and the number of employees affected. Focus your resources on addressing the highest-priority areas first.

Segment by Time and Resources

Once you've prioritized your gaps, determine what can be addressed now and what requires long-term planning. Some skills may be developed through quick training sessions or certifications, while others may need more extensive programs, mentorship, or hiring strategies.

Create a phased plan:

- Short-term: Fill immediate gaps affecting current performance.

- Mid-term: Upskill current staff in areas critical to next-phase growth.

- Long-term: Build future-ready capabilities aligned with industry trends.

Communicate and Take Action

Share your findings with leadership and team members to create transparency and gain support. Then, take action:

- Launch targeted training programs.

- Invest in learning and development platforms.

- Encourage mentorship and cross-training.

- Hire new talent to fill specialized gaps when necessary.

Conclusion

Identifying and prioritizing skills gaps is a proactive step toward building a stronger, more agile workforce. By aligning skills analysis with business strategy, assessing current capabilities, and focusing on high-impact areas, your organization can close gaps efficiently—and position itself for long-term success in a constantly evolving world.

Chapter Forty-Eight

Develop a Measurable Action Plan

I dentifying a skills gap within your organization is an important step—but recognizing the problem is only half the battle. To truly close these gaps and build a stronger, more competitive workforce, you need a clear and strategic skills gap analysis action plan that is measurable. This plan will help you move from insight to impact, equipping your team with the right capabilities to meet current demands and future challenges.

Here's a step-by-step guide on how to develop an effective action plan after conducting a skills gap analysis.

Review and Prioritize the Gaps

After completing your skills gap analysis, you should have a list of where your team or organization is falling short. But not all gaps are created equal.

Start by prioritizing the gaps based on factors such as:

- Business impact: Which skills are most critical to achieving your strategic goals?

- Urgency: Which gaps are affecting productivity, compliance, or customer satisfaction right now?

- Scope: Are the gaps widespread, or limited to a few individuals or teams?

Create a ranked list of the most important gaps to address. Focus on those that will bring the greatest return on investment or that pose the highest risk if left unresolved.

Set Clear Objectives

Once your priorities are set, define specific goals for addressing each skills gap. Use the SMART framework to make your objectives:

- Specific: Clearly state what you aim to achieve.

- Measurable: Determine how success will be evaluated.

- Achievable: Ensure goals are realistic, given your resources.

- Relevant: Aligns with organizational needs and priorities.

- Time-bound: Set deadlines for achieving each goal.

Example:
"Upskill all customer service representatives in conflict resolution techniques by the end of Q3 to reduce customer complaints by 20%."

Identify the Best Learning Methods

Now it's time to decide how you will close each skills gap. Different skills require different learning approaches. Options include:

- On-the-job training: Ideal for hands-on technical skills.

- Mentorship or coaching: Best for leadership or soft skills development.

- Online courses and certifications: Great for scalable, flexible learning.

- Workshops or classroom training: Useful for in-depth or collaborative learning.

- Cross-training: Helps develop multi-skilled teams and promotes internal mobility.

Choose learning methods that fit your workforce's learning styles, time availability, and existing knowledge levels.

Assign Roles and Responsibilities

A successful action plan requires clear ownership. Assign roles for:

- Program oversight: Who will manage the overall upskilling or reskilling initiative?

- Delivery: Who will lead the training sessions or coordinate external providers?

- Participation: Which employees need to be involved, and what are their expectations?

Ensure managers are also engaged in the process—they are crucial in reinforcing training, monitoring progress, and encouraging participation.

Allocate Resources

Determine what resources you need to execute the plan. Consider:

- Budget for training programs, technology, or external providers.

- Time employees will need to participate in learning activities.

- Technology platforms for tracking learning progress and hosting content.

- Personnel to facilitate or support the learning process.

Having a clear resource plan helps prevent delays and keeps your initiative on track.

Conclusion

A skills gap analysis is only valuable when followed by a clear and focused action plan. By prioritizing key gaps, setting measurable goals, choosing the right learning methods, and continuously monitoring progress, you can build a workforce that's not just prepared for today—but ready for the future. Investing in your people is one of the smartest decisions your organization can make—and a well-executed action plan ensures that investment pays off.

Chapter Forty-Nine

Implement the Action Plan in Phases

A skills gap analysis gives organizations critical insight into the difference between the skills their workforce currently has and the skills they need to achieve business goals. But simply identifying those gaps isn't enough. The real value comes from taking action—strategically and systematically. Implementing your skills gap analysis action plan in phases allows you to manage the process more effectively, reduce disruption, and maximize results.

Here's how to implement your action plan step by step, using a phased approach that ensures a lasting impact.

Phase 1: Planning and Preparation

Before jumping into training or recruitment efforts, you need a strong foundation. The planning phase sets the stage for everything to follow.

Key Actions:

- Review and validate your analysis: Confirm the gaps identified are accurate and aligned with business goals.

- Set priorities: Decide which gaps are most critical based on urgency, impact, and alignment with strategic objectives.

- Define success: Establish clear objectives and measurable outcomes for your action plan. For example, "Reduce production delays by upskilling 80% of line supervisors in workflow optimization within 6 months."

- Secure buy-in: Communicate the purpose and benefits of the plan to stakeholders, managers, and employees to ensure support and engagement.

Goal of Phase 1: Create a solid, actionable roadmap with leadership and team alignment.

Phase 2: Design and Resource Allocation

With a roadmap in place, it's time to design your solutions and allocate the necessary resources.

Key Actions:

- Select learning methods: Choose the most effective ways to close each skills gap (e.g., on-the-job training, online courses, workshops, mentoring, certifications).

- Assign responsibilities: Define who is responsible for managing and delivering each component of the plan.

- Allocate resources: Ensure sufficient budget, time, tools, and personnel are in place to support the implementation.

- Develop timelines and milestones: Establish a project timeline with realistic milestones for progress tracking.

Goal of Phase 2: Build a detailed and resourced implementation plan tailored to your organization's specific needs.

Phase 3: Pilot and Early Implementation

Rather than rolling out the entire plan all at once, start with a pilot program or a limited group. This allows you to test your approach, gather feedback, and make adjustments before full implementation.

Key Actions:

- Choose a test group: Select a department, role, or location with a manageable number of participants.

- Run the training or development activities: Deliver the planned learning experiences or interventions.

- Collect early feedback: Use surveys, assessments, or focus groups to evaluate engagement, learning outcomes, and initial impact.

- Make improvements: Refine content, delivery methods, or time-lines based on pilot feedback.

Goal of Phase 3: Validate the plan's effectiveness on a small scale and make informed adjustments.

Phase 4: Full-Scale Implementation

With lessons learned from the pilot, you're ready to roll out the action plan across the organization or target groups.

Key Actions:

- Launch in phases: Continue implementing in waves if necessary (e.g., by region, department, or job role) to manage capacity and ensure quality.

- Track participation and progress: Use learning management systems (LMS), performance data, and assessments to measure engagement and development.

- Support managers and employees: Provide ongoing communication, tools, and encouragement to keep teams motivated and on track.

Goal of Phase 4: Deliver consistent, scalable implementation with clear tracking and accountability.

Conclusion

Implementing a skills gap action plan in phases allows your organization to take a thoughtful, manageable, and results-driven approach to workforce development. By starting with planning and building through design, piloting, scaling, and optimizing, you can ensure every step delivers value. A phased implementation not only improves execution—it also builds confidence, engagement, and long-term capability across your team.

Chapter Fifty

Monitor, Evaluate, and Revise as Needed

A skills gap analysis should never be viewed as a one-time task. In today's dynamic and fast-paced work environment, technology changes, roles change, and new business needs emerge constantly. That's why it's essential to monitor, evaluate, and revise your skills gap analysis regularly.

Doing so ensures your workforce remains aligned with your goals, your training efforts stay relevant, and your organization stays competitive. Here's a step-by-step guide to monitoring, evaluating, and updating your skills gap analysis effectively.

Monitor Progress Regularly

Once you've implemented an action plan to address identified skill gaps, ongoing monitoring is crucial to track how things are progressing.

Key Monitoring Activities:

- Track training participation: Are employees engaging in the learning opportunities provided? Use Learning Management System (LMS) data or attendance records to monitor enrollment and completion.

- Measure performance improvements: Are employees applying new skills on the job? Review relevant performance metrics, productivity data, and quality indicators.

- Manager feedback: Supervisors are often the first to notice improvement—or a lack thereof—in employee performance. Schedule regular check-ins to gather insights.

- Employee self-assessments: Allow employees to reflect on their growth, which promotes ownership and provides another layer of feedback.

Monitoring keeps your plan on course and allows you to identify early signs of success—or areas that may require adjustment.

Evaluate the Impact of Your Action Plan

After a designated period (such as a quarter or six months), conduct a formal evaluation of your skills gap initiative. The goal is to assess whether your efforts are producing the desired outcomes.

Evaluation Questions to Ask:

- Have the targeted skills improved? Compare pre- and post-training assessments or performance evaluations.

- Have key business outcomes changed? Look at KPIs like productivity, error rates, sales performance, or customer satisfaction.

- Did the chosen training methods work? Evaluate the effectiveness of learning formats (e.g., in-person, online, mentorship).

- Were there any unintended outcomes? Sometimes, training can expose additional gaps or create role overlap. Document all findings.

Use a mix of quantitative (e.g., test scores, performance data) and qualitative (e.g., surveys, interviews) methods to get a comprehensive view.

Compare Against Evolving Business Needs

A successful organization is always evolving, and so are the skills required to support it. Even if your initial skills gap has been closed, new gaps may emerge due to:

- New technology or software adoption

- Changes in customer expectations or market trends

- Shifts in business strategies or company structure

- External factors like regulation changes or economic shifts

Review your organization's strategic goals regularly and assess whether your current workforce has the competencies to meet them. Align skills development efforts accordingly.

Revise the Skills Gap Analysis

Once you've evaluated the current status, it's time to revise the original skills gap analysis to reflect your updated findings. This might involve:

- Updating job role definitions and skill requirements

- Reassessing employee skill levels using updated tools or criteria

- Revising training plans to include newly identified needs

- Retiring outdated goals or approaches that are no longer relevant

Also, consider revising your skills matrix—a tool that maps employee skills to required competencies—so that it always reflects your organization's current state.

Communicate and Adapt Continuously

Keep lines of communication open with employees and leadership throughout the process. Share the progress being made, the impact of the initiatives, and what changes are being implemented.

Encourage a culture of continuous learning and adaptability where employees understand that developing new skills is not a one-time effort but an ongoing journey. This helps build buy-in and motivates team members to stay engaged.

Conclusion

Monitoring, evaluating, and revising your skills gap analysis ensures it stays relevant and effective in an ever-changing business environment. By treating it as a continuous cycle—not a one-time project—you empower your organization to remain agile, prepared, and competitive.

With regular updates and thoughtful analysis, your workforce can evolve alongside your goals, creating a foundation for long-term success.

www.ingramcontent.com/pod-product-compliance
Lightning Source LLC
Chambersburg PA
CBHW051522120626
46551CB00012B/1032